Joyful Possibilities

OCCUPYING THE SPACE "IN BETWEEN"
TO FIND A PATH THROUGH DIFFERENCE

by Susan Ferraro Smith

StreamlinePUBLISHING

Joyful Possibilities

OCCUPYING THE SPACE "IN BETWEEN"
TO FIND A PATH THROUGH DIFFERENCE

Copyright © 2020 by Susan Ferraro Smith

Cover design by Agnes Studio

Jeremy Jusek, Citations Editor

9 8 7 6 5 4 3 2 1

First Edition

Printed in the United States of America.

ISBN 978-1-7325191-7-6

Library of Congress Control Number: 2020915837

To my husband for his patience.

To my parents for their example.

To my children, the catalysts of my change.

Thank you from the bottom of my heart for your love, your patience, and your support as I have walked this frustrating and scintillating journey of faith and self-discovery. It is you who have shown me what love really means. It is your accompaniment on this journey of life that has been a sacred gift.

Contents

Acknowledgments

Thank you to all of my family and friends who consistently encouraged and supported me. With every act of kindness and love, you enriched my life in wonderful and significant ways. You have given me strength for the journey.

Thank you to our parish priest whose spiritual direction was just what I needed as I began a more directed journey to God.

Thank you to every person who has heard me speak - and told me of the speech's impact or suggested that I write a book. You confirmed that there was purpose in moving forward with this project.

Thank you to my current spiritual director who understands me, challenges me both intellectually and spiritually, and has been instrumental in helping me to find my way.

Thank you to the many people who read the draft of this book. Your questions provoked me to a deeper level of thought, your insights provided valuable guidance, and your edits created a more readable final product. I express my heartfelt gratitude for your honesty and your time.

Thank you to my citations editor and my publisher, without whose close attention to detail I would have been left floundering.

And thank you to the graphic artists who created the book's cover. You showed me, once again, that when I move myself out of the way to make room for others, the result is more meaningful than I could have imagined.

Preface

The individual threads of my life - personal longings, relationships, work, motherhood - sought unity that ultimately could only be found in God who expanded my vision, softened the rough edges of my controlling tendencies, unlocked the power of my heart, and nudged me onto a path toward coherence. Questions began to have answers. Restless searching and fighting to satisfy personal desires and expectations lessened as I began to find comfort in the arms of Jesus, peace in the truths of life, and wholeness in the spiritual wellsprings of God.

The journey of faith that brought me closer to God helped me to better understand myself. And as God moved my soul and fashioned my heart in incremental but significant ways, he became a powerful presence in my life. Notwithstanding uncertainty and angst in the midst of that movement, God's love revealed joyful possibilities along the way that fueled my path forward. (Part I)

The journey of faith that brought me closer to God also prompted a parallel journey that brought me closer to the people in my life. When I was willing to set aside certainty and control and walk into that space "in between" the opposites - whether between my humanity and God's divinity or between opposite people, ideas, or expectations - my vision was expanded, my understanding was broadened, and I was able to see the picture differently. There, in the space "in between," diversity was a powerful vehicle for discovering roots that unite. And there, in that space "in between," I found joyful possibilities - and a God whose patience and love provided every needed grace for the journey. (Part II)

To know my journey requires knowing the journey of both my heart *and* my head, and my head has often wrestled with one question in particular: who *are* we as human beings? I find the question to be compelling and in need of urgent attention. Hate between and among human beings is abundant, spewed forth personally, socially, and politically, and manifested in the violence that has become all too common in our society. If these actions represent who we really are as human beings, our path forward appears bleak, but if these actions are *not* representative of who we are as human beings, then we must assume the responsibility of changing course. Although Part III may seem like a diversion from my personal story, it is an essential part of my journey because it incorporates theological, philosophical, historical, and experiential lessons about our humanity which have helped to clarify my path. (Part III)

Prayer, self-reflection, Scripture, and church were some of my pathways to God, and during life's challenges, I received five messages of hope and possibility that strengthened me for the journey. The Holy Spirit evoked a burning desire within me that found its satisfaction in God's love. Part I's journal entries of restlessness became Part IV's journal entries of trust - and joyful possibilities were made real. (Part IV)

PART I: THE CALL

To what are you calling me, oh God?
Why do you create such a yearning within me?
You, the Creator of the universe; I, the mere created.
What do you want with me?
I hear you, but I do not know what you are saying.
You move my soul, but my mind is perplexed.
You demand my attention, but I am impotent in response.
Why such desire when there is no satisfaction?[1]

---

1   The italicized words that begin each Part are the words of this author.

CHAPTER ONE

Paving the Way

The words at the beginning of Part 1 represent my angst in trying to follow the call that I felt deep within me. It was bold and insistent, and I knew that I had no choice but to follow it, but it was also unsettling and disconcerting because I wanted to be in control and cling to understanding. As time passed, however, the call took its rightful place, perhaps because it was so authentic to my life. It embraced me as I was, where I was, and used my inherent interests to spark me along the way. Ultimately, the call moved me on a journey toward a greater understanding of myself, my family, and my God. It led me to change, to a place where faith *in* God would become relationship *with* God, and to a space of wholeness "in between" the opposites. It placed me on a path forward that had begun in my past.

* * *

My parents embodied the gospel values of love, hospitality, and charity. They celebrated life and opened their home to family and friends with food, music, and laughter. My siblings and I worked in the bakery that my parents owned, and routinely our parents would tell us to give a customer a box of cookies - or a box of donuts - or a loaf of bread - or *something*. My parents were generous to those in need and those with plenty, to stranger and friend alike; generosity was simply part of their nature. My mother always told me that the more she gave, the more she received. Not long after her death, I asked our young son what he most remembered about her and he said, "She gave me everything she had." Truth spoken from the mouth of a child.

My dad was raised in poverty in a very small town in southern Italy. He remembers that when his mother made bread, she would save some of the dough (the "starter dough") to give to her neighbor, who would also save the starter dough and pass it on to the next neighbor, until the starter dough would return to my grandmother and the process would begin anew. Mother Teresa tells about taking a bowl of rice to a family that was in dire need of food. Before even feeding her children, the recipient took half of the rice to the neighboring family who had also been without food for a number of days.[2] The poor know how to share and they do it willingly and lovingly. My dad always remembered his poverty, and he honored that memory as he and my mother poured out their generosity on all who had the pleasure of passing their way.

Lessons about generosity also brought lessons about gratitude and the necessity of saying thank you for all of the kindnesses that had been bestowed upon us. Delivering baked goods to show appreciation or writing notes to recognize a kindness were two of the many ways that my parents said "thank you." They taught me that an expression of gratitude is an expression of love as it honors and respects the giver.

My parents were also supportive of me and provided an environment in which I could learn and grow. When I was about eight years old, I wanted to learn how to "ring up" on the cash

---

2 González-Balado, J.L. (1997). *Mother Teresa - Her Life, Her Work, Her Message.* Liguori Publications.

register, so they found a crate for me to stand on, taught me what to do, and when it was time for a customer to pay, my mother recited the prices as I pushed the register's buttons. I felt so special. And when I wanted to bring my classmates to the bakery for a tour, not only did my parents agree, but every child went home with a bag of goodies that my mother had lovingly packed. I felt so proud. And when I wanted to have a lemonade stand outside the bakery doors in the summer, room was made for my entrepreneurial attempts. I felt so grown up.

But none of these examples is meant to convey that I always got what I wanted. My parents encouraged desire for the "right" things and deterred desire for the "wrong" things. I was free to work hard and pursue individual interests and talents, but I was never free to be lazy or entitled. As a teenager, I was unhappy that I had to go to school Monday through Friday *and* work at the bakery on Saturday and Sunday mornings. I complained to my dad about having no day to sleep in, but he explained that the bakery was our family's business, it provided a livelihood that we enjoyed, and none of us was entitled to its benefits without its costs. My parents were teaching me about love and responsibility. They were teaching me that unconditional love did not mean unconditional freedom and that the standard of conduct to which I was expected to adhere required consideration of more than myself. They were teaching me about the necessity of broadening my vision to understand that benefit *and* cost, self *and* family, freedom *and* responsibility produce a different result together than any one of them is capable of producing alone.

Their lessons about rights, responsibilities, and relationships also included the lesson that sometimes people do not act in optimal ways. For a time, my parents owned a grocery store adjacent to the bakery, and theft was an occasional problem. My dad would meet with the offender (and, depending on age, his/her parents), and together they would reach a resolution that usually included both restitution and a lesson in responsibility. There was no cynicism. Just matter-of-fact protection of property and insistence on adherence to a moral code.

My parents' moral code was the Golden Rule: "[d]o to others whatever you would have them do to you" (Matt 7:12, Saint Joseph Edition of the New American Bible). In fact, stories about Jesus were regularly woven into my dad's lessons of life. He often said, "You have to suffer to get to Paradise." He would tell me that I need not try to please everyone because "if Jesus couldn't do it, you won't be able to do it either." My dad believed that every person must follow that unique calling that is his/hers alone, one that can be discovered in what brings us joy, and to this day, his mantra is "Don't worry. Do what you can and let go of the rest."

I am blessed to have grown up in a nurturing home where responsible, loving parents cared for me, wanted what was best for me, and guided me in the ways of life. Because they showed me how rights, responsibilities, and relationships could be appropriately "balanced," I felt empowered to engage in that same balancing act. There was no need to be afraid of what life had to offer because I had been furnished with the tools necessary to do the work. And now I can see that my parents' empowering love, which made me feel safe and worthy, set the groundwork for the journey of change about which I now write, a journey which brought me full circle by confirming what my parents had taught me: that responsible love will pave the way to meaning and goodness, and that forging a path through the contrasts is part of our life's work.

* * *

As I got older, I embraced what seemed to be another set of contrasts as I studied my two favorite subjects: math and literature. While many were surprised that I embraced both "left-brained" and "right-brained" subjects that encompassed the objective analysis of math and the subjective world of relationship, I realize now that neither subject can be so clearly delineated. They are complements more than opposites. They represent thought and feeling, predictability and uncertainty, clarity and confusion, and both subjects require delicate and refined movement toward a more complete whole.

Movement through difference was also important in my work as a lawyer, but it is interesting to note that I was much more comfortable with objective analysis than subjective relationship. For most of my career, I worked with corporate contracts. The parties' opposing interests required that we find workable solutions through difference, and we did so through the process of negotiation: the parties gave up what was less important to receive what was more important. Decisions of the head guided us through.

When I handled family law matters early in my career, however, I had a different, and more emotional, experience. In custody matters, I would awaken in the middle of the night in a sweat-inducing fear that I had lost my own children - at a time when I wasn't even a mother. Trying to do what was best for the children didn't always include an easy definition of "best," and even when the "best" was outlined, sadness and loss were not magically wiped away. "Getting" and "giving up" were not so easy in matters of the heart. The path was much less definitive, the pain much more palpable, and I quickly learned that I was happier working in the business arena.

But the lessons of complementarity and wholeness are important ones; they teach me that life cannot be neatly compartmentalized. Addressing the issues that arise in my relationships requires a necessary amalgamation of both emotion *and* conscious decision-making. It requires an encounter with misunderstanding and hurt, which can be emotionally exhausting, and it requires making the decision to become a more loving human being through the difficult work of *change.*

During my journey of faith, I found myself in the midst of much difference - but change was not my desired end. I was "fine." My faith was "fine." I went to church and I prayed to God. My prayers, however, consisted of my talking, with no consideration given to listening, and I hadn't fully experienced God so as to know what was possible. In fact, when I heard a story about a hospitalized man who kept an empty chair by his bed for Jesus, and died with his head resting on the chair, I did not understand. How could a human ever be that close to Jesus? Who would try?[3]

---

3   *The Empty Chair.* (2020). Jaredstory.com. Retrieved June 2020, from http://www.jaredstory.com/empty_chair.html

CHAPTER TWO

Life-Changing Experiences

It was motherhood that most startlingly rocked my world. But motherhood did not come easily. Something that my husband and I had taken for granted as a natural part of life seemed not to be so natural after all. But then, when we least expected it, I was expectant and our son was born - when we were married almost fifteen years. My husband's words as he held our baby for the first time best reflect the experience. He said, "It's like touching God." A perfect sentence for those times in life when God's divinity imbues our humanity. A perfect sentence for those times in life when complete and unconditional love of another swoops down upon us, overtakes us, and embraces us in its everlasting goodness. A perfect sentence for those times in life when thought and emotion fuse, push us to the limits of human creativity and possibility, and grant us the grace of glimpsing the Divine. Then when we were married almost twenty-two years, God's very real presence poured out again in the birth of our daughter, and life's magnificence was once again revealed in mystery. Perhaps I was moving one step closer to understanding how someone could reach out to an "empty" hospital chair.

I fell head over heels in love with these children, felt an overwhelming desire to be with them, and felt a gripping responsibility to teach them. Their lives exposed some very pure and raw truth about my own and awakened my heart with a kind of love I did not know existed. Although I had felt the immense love of my own parents, until I became a parent I had no means of accurately grasping the scope of that love. The big questions of life I had pondered so diligently in literature classes began to surface once again. Who were these children to become as human beings? What was my role as their mother? How could I best help them understand what is really important in life? How could I help them to know God?

I sought answers with an expectation of teaching my children, but, instead, the questions propelled me on my own journey of self-discovery, a journey in which I would sometimes be the student in the classroom of life taught by my children. These questions set me on a journey in which love would push itself to the foreground and powerfully strengthen the voice of my heart. My children provoked within me a solemn and devout longing to be the kind of responsible parent that my own parents had modeled.

* * *

Motherhood prompted more frequent and more fervent prayer - in gratitude for our children's lives and in prayerful hope for their well-being - and it elicited within me a deep commitment to passing on our faith to our children. I home-schooled our son in religious education for a time, but teaching theology from a book was an intellectual pursuit not well-suited to understanding either God's mysteries or faith's meaningful connections to life. I tried to make those connections by sharing my own experiences, but often my relatively superficial knowledge left both of us dissatisfied. I wanted more. Perhaps my inadequacy prompted need for more; perhaps it was simply the right time in my life to take a deeper plunge. In either event, I felt a compelling need to better understand faith and its relevance to our lives, and I felt a compelling need to write. I wrote about how God created each of us to be unique and special and how God calls each of us to very unique tasks. I wrote about responsibility, truth, friends, mistakes, and prayer, and I entitled this essay "Know Who You Are." The writing energized me, and I could not wait for an hour here or there to work on it. The more I wrote, the more passionate I became.

During this time, our son played baseball and because we baseball moms talked regularly about faith and the challenges of raising children, I shared my writing with them. The other moms thought I should use it to do something with young people at church. I thought so too, and confirmation of a possible tangible result fueled me even more. The forceful compulsion to write and the joy it elicited in me were incredibly meaningful; I felt certain this writing had a purpose, and I looked forward to seeing it fulfilled. I sought guidance from some of the people who taught religious education classes at our church, but they thought the essay was too complex. I considered what I could do with the essay, but nothing materialized, so with great frustration and disappointment, I set the essay aside. I didn't understand why I had so much energy and enthusiasm for something that would ultimately end up on a shelf. One thing was certain: God was calling me to something *but I did not know what.*

* * *

One day, on my way to meet a client, I listened to a radio interview with Rafe Esquith, a Los Angeles inner city school teacher, that moved me deeply. That afternoon, I bought his book, *There Are*

No Shortcuts. Feeling an overwhelming connection with him, I could not put the book down. What he thought as a teacher, I thought as a mother and had tried to incorporate into my essay. Reading the book became an all-encompassing experience for me. I kept asking: Why did I have a meeting that day? Why had I listened to that particular radio station? Why was the book evoking so much emotion in me? *Why?*

I suspected that the emotion was conveying a message, but the message was far from clear. Perplexed, irritated, and angry, I reached the point where I had had "enough." If God was calling me, then he needed to help me understand. I put the book down and spoke to him very loudly and emotionally: *"What am I supposed to learn from this? What are you telling me? Tell me because I am not getting it!"* I wondered why I was wasting my time on what felt like an insincere invitation to a party that was never going to happen, yet I was determined to sit back down and try again. I picked up the book, turned to the new chapter I was about to begin, only to discover that it was entitled "On the Road to Find Out." And in the third sentence of that chapter, the author wrote: " . . . I knew that the most important thing in teaching and parenting (and life) is to *know who you are*" (my emphasis).[4] Okay, God, I hear you. Thank you. I don't know what I am supposed to do, but perhaps I am at least on the right track . . . .[5]

---

4   Esquith, R. (2003). *There Are No Shortcuts.* Anchor Books. p. 94.

5   Interestingly, when I recently looked at the book to check the reference, I was even more moved by the author's subsequent sentences. After saying that the most important thing is to know who you are, he wrote: "I just hadn't found the answer . . . I just knew I could never be a good teacher without defining myself . . . ." *That* is why I connected to him. I also could not be a good teacher to my children without defining myself in the context of my God. I simply didn't know it then.

* * *

Although I periodically found myself "on the right track," I still did not know where I was going and that aimlessness caused me great consternation. At one of our church missions, having heard the words "spiritual advisor" frequently, I began to wonder if such a person could help me through this process of discernment. I talked with the priest at our church, and in one of the many examples of God's grace in my life, he agreed to be my spiritual advisor. Knowing I loved to write, he recommended I begin the process of journaling - and writing became a part of my daily routine. After many months, something unsettling happened: I ran into one of the baseball moms who had read my essay years before, and one of the first things she asked me was what I had ever done with it. I had to sheepishly admit that I had done nothing. I could not wait to convey that conversation to our priest, as evidence that I was going nowhere and making no progress. But when I did, without missing a beat, he said, "What are you *doing* with it? You're *living* it!"

But I did not think living it was enough. Something was not right, and I felt the need to do more. My uneasiness grew into an incessant nagging, a restlessness, a sense that I was not where I was supposed to be. One of my journal entries reads: "Self-awareness and soul-searching are gut-wrenching and agonizing." How could I be searching if I did not know what I was searching *for?*

I longed for order to return to my life. The confusion I was experiencing was unnerving and now, it was moving to a new level. I was feeling a steady and profound uneasiness with the way things were in my professional life. I had loved practicing law for many years, but now something was different. I felt like I was not using my gifts in the best way possible. I continued to feel a call to do "something else," but I could not define "something else." Our priest cautioned me against making big, bold moves. He reminded me that I did not have to leave the practice of law in order to serve God. Perhaps, he suggested, I could move from corporate law to social justice law. But from experiences I had had in my early years of legal practice, that path did not seem the best one for me. So the struggle continued. I found myself straddling law and "something else" and not totally immersed in either. I felt fragmented and disingenuous and knew that it was time to leave the profession I loved, the community of professionals I cherished, and the identity I had known for so long.

To what are you calling me, oh God?
To the unknown which I loathe?
How do I follow? Where do I go?

* * *

I decided to fuel the two passions within me: to serve children and to further my education. I joined the Christ Child Society, a nonprofit organization that serves children in need, and began a Master of Arts in Humanities program that enabled me to study the big questions of life through the disciplines of theology, philosophy, and literature. In these new ventures, I would look for God at every turn.

During this time, with no intention on my part, I found myself reflecting on my high school years, wanting to thank my high school friends for always being so kind and supportive of me. Every morning on a walk, "out of the blue" a speech would begin to unfurl in my head: "If I accomplished anything, it was because of you . . . ." I didn't understand why this speech kept coming to mind. Although I would have been happy to share my thoughts with my classmates, it was unlikely that I would ever speak in front of them again.

Also around this time I celebrated a milestone birthday, and the following weekend we were to meet my family for a Mother's Day dinner in our small home town. During the days between my birthday and the dinner, my journal reflects restlessness:

"Why am I not content? Doesn't the Spirit give each person a gift to be used for the common good? What is my gift? I don't know. These days it doesn't seem like I have any gifts that can be used for anything. I must pray for help in seeing what God wants me to see. Help me, Lord. Help me to know why you created me. What am I supposed to do to leave this world a better place? What am I capable of doing? Please help me to know."

The weekend came, and we drove to dinner. It turns out, however, that the dinner was simply a ruse for a surprise birthday party for me. My sister, my husband's sister, and my best friend from high school had planned it. I was overwhelmed, and the events of that evening were life-altering. One by one, people talked about what I had done to impact their lives. They told me I articulated feelings in a way that binds me with others and I lived life intentionally. They told me how my notes to them were meaningful, how my sacrifice for family was significant, how my ability to bring family together was enriching. I couldn't believe what I was hearing. I didn't know I had done anything to impact their lives. It felt more like a eulogy than a birthday party. I felt so loved, like being wrapped in a warm blanket with everyone smiling at me. Through my family and friends, the questions I had asked just a few days before were being answered. Our priest had been right: I didn't have to do anything "big" with the essay I had written. I was living it – and my family and friends were telling me how they had reaped the benefits.

I was humbled beyond measure, full of love and gratitude. Somewhat dazed, having no idea what to say, I cried, stood up, walked to the microphone, and without any thought said, "If I have done anything good, it is because of you," and I gave the speech I had given so many times to my imagined classmates. Later, our priest reminded me that God prepared me for my birthday party, just as he prepares me every day for what lies ahead.

Father Jacques Philippe, a French priest who followed a call to the priesthood after studying mathematics and doing scientific research,[6] admonishes us to listen:

". . . to the calls, the discrete, mysterious invitations that come to us continuously throughout life . . . Sometimes they come through experiences or by the example of others who touch us, sometimes from desires that arise in our hearts or requests from people who are close to us, often from Holy Scripture. They originate from God, who gives us life, never ceases to watch over us, and wants tenderly to lead and constantly intervene for each of his children in a way that is discreet, often imperceptible, yet efficacious."[7]

And Father Alfred Delp, a Jesuit priest who remained loyal to his own call, even to the point of execution in 1945, wrote: "What really matters is the fact that we are called and we must be sufficiently awake to hear the call."[8] I realize now that I was sufficiently awake to hear the call. The knocking was loud and clear. The problem

6   Philippe, J. (2020) *About Father Jacques Philippe.* Fr. Jacques Philippe. Retrieved June 2020, from https://www.frjacquesphilippe.com/about
7   Philippe, J. (2008). *Called to Life.* (Carter, N., Trans.). Scepter Publishers, Inc. pp. 2-3.
8   Delp, A. (2004). *Prison Writings.* Orbis Books. p. 79.

was not being called; the problem was *following*. Jesus tells us that the Spirit is like the wind: it "blows where it wills, and you can hear the sound it makes, but you do not know where it comes from or where it goes" (John 3:8). That kind of unpredictable movement was the total opposite of me, a stubborn, strong-willed woman who wanted to be in control.

I had begun a fervent and arduous journey in which I was, from time to time, a combatant. While I had a piercing and penetrating thirst for "something more," I also had a deep longing to cling mightily to earthly understanding and control. I wanted a measurable and logical route to a known end. It was okay to be called by God - as long as I could lead the way. But therein lies the difficulty in responding to a call from God: its nature cannot be apprehended; its means cannot be ascertained; and its end cannot necessarily be understood. It is mystery.

CHAPTER THREE

Slow Movement Forward

During the years that I volunteered at the Christ Child Society and took classes, my desire for knowledge and my desire to help others were satisfied. And raising children was a gift that nourished my soul. For a time, I felt a sense of satisfaction that I was doing just what I was supposed to do. But toward the end of my master's program, restlessness returned. What was I supposed to *do*? My husband couldn't understand why I found no satisfaction in what I *was* doing, and my spiritual advisor, who now was someone other than our priest, said one day in exasperation, "Susan, *when are you going to become what you already are?*" Although I could understand the question, what did it mean in terms of mapping out a plan?

I was obviously still looking for some tangible result consistent with my expectations. I was learning more about myself, but what was my job supposed to be? I left the practice of law intending to transition to different work but still had no idea what that work would be. Every suggestion I received from those around me just did not seem right. It was a difficult time. I felt like a failure, well aware of the fact that it was taking me so long to move so little. I needed to respond to God's call in faith, but the requisite action eluded me.

I sought. I searched. I pursued. With spiritual direction. With self-reflection. With prayer, daily Mass, and Scripture. I regularly sat in the Eucharistic Chapel of our church writing about the readings, meditations, and gospel stories to which I was drawn. I thought about them in the context of my own life experience and began to internalize the words and concepts in a way that created room for movement of the Spirit within my heart. I often asked myself why I was feeling so much dissatisfaction. Was I causing it? Was it coming from a place of arrogance within me? Did I want "more" of something material? But I could never uncover a personal motive. In truth, I did not have any control over this restlessness. It was there, it was not my doing, and I could not ignore it even if I wanted to. I hated that it placed me right in the middle of confusion and uncertainty, a place so intolerable for the rational me who wanted to understand everything.

Four months before the conclusion of classes, my journal reflects angst:

"Now with graduate school coming to an end, I am again feeling lost. I say that I only want to serve you, but then why am I dissatisfied with serving you as I have, as I am?"

Later that month I had an interesting experience while walking past the Eucharistic Chapel in our church. I was thinking about conscience, the subject of my final paper, and I felt drawn to return to the chapel and go in, so I did. I began to cry but wasn't sure of the reason. What was moving me? I asked God to write on my soul, as he would write in sand. But I asked that God's writing never be washed away like the writing in sand. And immediately, the words in my mind were clear: "You have to know who you are." I started crying again. I have to follow my conscience to be who I really am. I was deeply moved.

But in truth, I was not ready to accept who I really was. One day in a meeting with my spiritual advisor and then again at the dinner table that evening with my family, I vented my very deep frustration:

"I am tired of this process. It started nine years ago. This gnawing. This inner unsettledness. I worked so hard in my master's program. I loved it. And it changed me for the better. Maybe I am disappointed that a clear path to a job is not opening up. I want a productive job that I feel good about. At what point do I say this is not the right path?"

I was frustrated because I was hearing a word - over and over - that I did not want to hear. My husband had asked me if I wanted to be a minister. After one of my speeches, a person in the audience suggested that I become an Episcopalian minister. And on the day of my deep frustration at the dinner table, my spiritual advisor's voice was again about ministry. I envisioned ministry as formal work in an organized church and that did not seem the right path for me. All I could do was cry. I did not want to be a minister . . . .

Interestingly, our priest had previously told me that ministry is all about process. I wasn't happy to hear that either. I had always been results-oriented: grades in the academic world, completing the work I set out to do on behalf of my clients in the legal world, and some tangible success with my essay. Process seemed like a path leading nowhere. But two months before I finished my graduate work, a change within me was evident: I was beginning to exhibit a new understanding of the value of the process, the value of the journey. My journal entry reads:

"I want to journey with you, God. The journey changes me. I see things differently. I don't jump in to act quite as forcefully. I react differently to others. I feel different. You have moved my heart. That I know. I am quieter toward others, gentler I think. Sometimes it's all very mixed up. I would like it to be less so. Perhaps at this point it has to be mixed up."

* * *

Then one day, as I worked on my final paper for graduate school the phone rang, and a friend asked if I would be the keynote speaker for a hospice grounds dedication. "Of course," I told her. I loved to speak. During my adult life I had spoken at a Christian lay breakfast and other events, and I had spoken frequently in my capacity as a lawyer. As a matter of fact, approximately thirty years prior to that phone call, I had actually told my husband that if I could have any job at all, I would choose to be a public speaker.

The hospice grounds dedication speech was well received and I was very happy. My spiritual advisor encouraged me to speak any time and every time I was asked. He gave me wonderful advice when he said, "Every time you write a speech, you will further refine what you think. And every time you give a speech, your audience will tell you whether there is a need to hear what you have to say."

A couple of weeks later, I received another phone call. This one was from the president of the National Christ Child Society (who was a member of our local chapter). She said she was acting outside of her comfort zone, that she had prayed and prayed and that my name kept coming into her mind. She asked if I would be the keynote speaker for the National Christ Child Society convention that fall. Of course, I accepted the invitation.

Writing the speech refined my thoughts as my spiritual advisor had predicted, and after delivering the speech, the audience gave a very clear indication that they had been touched in some way. While those two speaking engagements did not miraculously shape a future path, they opened many doors to subsequent speaking engagements which have moved me forward. I was beginning to realize that I could have impact on others when I combined both theory *and* experience, both head *and* heart. Theoretically and practically, God's call seemed to be moving me, once again, on a journey through the opposites.

CHAPTER FOUR

God's Hand

I was beginning to recognize God's hand in my life. My thoughts, my feelings, and the events of my life were merging in ways that caused me to see differently. I could look back, with a bit more objectivity, and see that a loving, gentle, gracious, merciful, and very patient God was traveling this journey of life with me. I was beginning to inherently trust that God would never leave me. It was the beginning of a kind of relationship with God that at an earlier time I could not have envisioned. It was one more step in the direction of reaching out to an "empty" hospital chair.

Eighteen years ago I could not have written meaningfully on the subject of "knowing who you are" because I had yet to understand myself more fully. I could not have written much about God without first *experiencing* God more deeply. Perhaps I was not able to find solace in our priest's statement that I was living my essay because I was, in fact, being required to do more than that: I was being required to internalize the lessons, change, and make the connections so I could ultimately explain them. I also now see the irony of falling so emotionally in love with the book *There Are No Shortcuts*. Because there are no shortcuts. The work of wholeness, connection, and unity requires the journey of an entire lifetime.

Eighteen years ago my "Know Who You Are" essay about God, self-knowledge, and relationships, would have been an objective shortcut with this message to its readers: "Come to me and I will *show you how.*" Today, having found a space somewhere between my head and my heart, the message is a bit different: "Come to me and *we will walk this path together.*" It is the difference between result and process, between changing others and being changed myself. It is about opening my life to joyful possibilities, to the mysteries of God, and moving forward anew. It *is* about ministry, one which I am now ready to wholeheartedly embrace.

PART II:
THE "IN BETWEEN"

The curtain is pulled back.
I occupy a larger space.
I am alive with joyful possibility.
I am not diminished, but whole.
I am not alone, but connected.
I am alive with joyful possibility.
I see more; I see differently.
I see truth in unity.
I am alive with joyful possibility.

.

CHAPTER FIVE

Jesus' Commandment to Love

Opening my life to the mysteries of God and moving forward anew require authenticity of self and truth of relationship with other, both of which can be difficult and disconcerting. But Jesus provides a road map. When he was asked to name the most important commandment, he said: "You shall love the Lord, your God, with all your heart, with all your soul, and with all your mind . . . . The second is like it: You shall love your neighbor as yourself" (Matt 22:37-39). Jesus asks us to embrace the contrasts of heart, mind, and soul, to embrace the contrasts of God, neighbor, and self, and to walk *through* these contrasts in a movement of *love*.

How do we even begin to comply with such a difficult commandment? Individual will, neighbor's will, and God's will are not always in sync with one another; emotions and thoughts often race in different directions. Finding a path through that kind of conflict can be very difficult; finding a path through *lovingly* can seem impossible.

I have discovered that my struggle to be the best human being I can be lies in between the polarities - between what *I* want and what *you* want - in the space where we can discover what *we* want. To carry out Jesus' commandment to love, I must explore not only self, other, and God, but also the space in between. Here, in this space, the interests of self *and* the interests of other can be embraced *and* challenged in a continual assimilation of opposites toward some kind of sustainable balance.

CHAPTER SIX

Facing My Faults

During the first year of my more directed spiritual journey, during that first year of prayer, self-reflection, journaling, discernment, and regular meetings with our priest, I found myself struggling as I came face to face with the opposites within myself: my gifts *and my faults.* Every time I was angry with my husband and knew exactly what he had done wrong, I immediately saw in my mind's eye a time when I had done the exact same thing I was angry at him for doing. It happened to me every time, for an entire year. My faults loomed in front of me; I began to see where I was intolerant and hard to live with. It wasn't pleasant by any stretch of the imagination, but it most certainly was necessary for me to move forward. Interestingly, however, the process of self-awareness never caused me to fall so low as to lose my self-worth. I always knew that God loved me in spite of my faults. My faults didn't need to define me; they simply needed to make me less arrogant and closed-minded.

During this journey of attempted understanding of difference, I found a place of sameness, a place of equalization where we are *all* human, where we *all* have wonderful gifts and we *all* have challenging faults. Instead of being embarrassed by my faults, I was empowered to try to change them. I discovered that acknowledging my own fallibility enabled me to envision something new: how my husband might see me, and it was not a pretty picture. Was I really that judgmental, seeing the splinter in my husband's eye without seeing the wooden beam in my own? (See Matt 7:5).

I felt unsettled and vulnerable. Ultimately, I concluded that I did not like this part of myself. I began to look at where I was and consider where I could be. The questions became clear: Who am I? Who do I want to become? How do I get there? Arrogant righteousness about my husband's shortcomings began to melt away in the face of my own failings. Indignation and exasperation turned into gratitude that he had actually tolerated me all these years. My view of my husband had shifted, and in the process so did my view of myself.

And I didn't like it. I didn't like being at fault; it was so much easier being angry at someone else. The world as I knew it was shifting - away from me and toward others; it brought with it a lot of wrestling, a lot of crying, and a lot of discomfort in no longer feeling powerfully safe in my own opinion. I was experiencing the turmoil of transformation.

Through prayer and honest self-reflection, the Spirit moved me beyond my self to the space between me and my husband. In that messy space between, I found the footing to which I could cling when difference began to unsteady me. I found unity in our common humanity. There, I began to see myself more authentically and began to see the relationship between my husband and me more truthfully. There, different and more complete views chiseled away the anger that comes with imbalance and made room for the dignity and respect that emanate from sameness. There, the mutuality necessary for relationships to flourish began to unfold.

CHAPTER SEVEN

The Challenge of Martha & Mary

But the process of honestly knowing and understanding myself was merely beginning. I had yet to more fully understand the gospel story of Martha and Mary. I had heard this story many times and never liked what I heard. I am a Martha, a woman of action, and I had very little patience for Mary, the contemplative. The following is the passage from Luke10:38-42, along with my commentary (in bold) about how I used to read it:

"As they continued their journey [Jesus] entered a village where a woman whose name was Martha welcomed him. **[Yes, I can relate to Martha. I welcome people when they come to my community or my home.]** She had a sister named Mary [who] sat beside the Lord at his feet listening to him speak. **[Already, I am not so sure about this Mary. She is *sitting*. I am a do-er and I relate to action more than non-action.]** Martha, burdened with much serving, came to him and said, 'Lord, do you not care that my sister has left me by myself to do the serving? Tell her to help me.' **[Yes, yes, yes, yes, yes! I understand you, Martha. I have been there. There is so much to be done - and *where is everyone?*]** The Lord said to her in reply, 'Martha, Martha, you are anxious and worried about many things. There is need of only one thing. Mary has chosen the better part and it will not be taken from her.'" **[*Mary* has chosen the better part? I am doing all the work to feed and serve people, to take care of them, and *Mary* has the better part?]**

I didn't understand. I was working hard and trying to make everyone feel welcome, yet I felt like I was being scolded. Luckily, however, a homily by our priest provided me with another vantage point. He said that Martha and Mary were not either/or; they were both/and. He said that everyone has to *do* something from time to time and everyone has to *sit with Jesus* from time to time. That made a lot of sense to me, so I began to explore my own strong Martha tendencies.

* * *

I hesitate to share my parenting stories because every family is different, with its unique strengths and weaknesses, personalities and temperaments, circumstances and challenges. What might be right for my family might not be right for another. My tendency to control means that learning to let go is a necessary part of my journey; the same may not be true for others. I share my experiences, nonetheless, because these experiences as a parent have brought me face to face with parts of myself that I needed to see, with that "in between" space I needed to experience, with the power of God's love.

In the years I practiced law, my analytical skills, my "take charge" attitude, and my efficiency stood me in good stead. How surprised I was, then, to discover that these skills did not facilitate my parenting; in fact they sometimes frustrated it. My Martha "take charge" attitude became a controlling attitude: *"I'll do it; I'll show you how . . . ."* My efficiency became expedience: "You'll finish faster if you do it *this* way . . . ." And my analytical skills, my ability to identify every possible problem imaginable - so valuable when protecting legal clients - made me an overly protective parent.

Our son was in his teen years, years that very often place parents and children in conflict. My Martha would *act* and say exactly what she thought when she thought it - and later regret having said it. I came to realize that our son was reacting to my statements by feeling badly, something that was not my intention at all. My husband (my Mary, my diverse voice) gave me good advice. He said, "You can always say what you want to say in the morning after sleeping on it." I thought a lot about that statement and tried very hard to be more patient, more understanding of my son's viewpoint, less dogmatic. While my journals are replete with examples of how I fell short, I share an example of when I succeeded because it illustrates how the combination of Mary's contemplation *and* Martha's action can lead to unity even in the midst of conflict.

To understand my story, you have to know that my Martha is not very flexible. She likes to be in control and does not like uncertainty. She loves to learn, loves academics, thinks that education is an invaluable asset in life, and thinks that everyone should fall into that line and march accordingly. So when our fifteen-year-old son (who had been in a rock band since the seventh grade) told me that his dream job was to tour with a band, I was taken aback. He said that if he had the "opportunity of a lifetime" to go on tour after high school, he might choose to do that instead of going to college. I was not jumping for joy. "I might not want a job like yours or dad's," he said. (I practiced law at the time and my husband is an investment advisor.) My emotions and thoughts were racing. I knew exactly what I wanted to say, and my Martha was ready to say it.

But through this process of prayer, self-reflection, and discernment I had somehow, by the grace of God, moved from the black-and-white world of my Martha to the various shades of

Martha/Mary gray, so I withheld the words. Instead, I asked myself, "What do I say? How do I guide him?" My journal entry captures the essence of our conversation:

I said I love you for who you are, not because you are a good student, not because you are a good athlete, not because of what kind of job you will have. Your dad and I will always encourage you to get an education because we believe it is an important part of life. But we can't live your life for you. If you have an opportunity of a lifetime, you should take it. Everyone should take that one opportunity of a lifetime. But school must remain a priority. You have many gifts; you will have lots of options. School work must be kept up.

I don't care about saying that my son is a doctor or a lawyer. That doesn't matter to me. What matters to me is that you do something good with your life, that you do what God wants you to do. Pray. Ask God for guidance; work to do his will. That's what's important.

I told him several times how much I loved him. I cried a lot. I said he was God's gift to us. That letting go is very hard for me as a parent. That I have asked for God's help in doing what is right. That I have tried to work on my faults but sometimes they nonetheless loom over me. That I probably would not have been able to have had this conversation a year ago.

He thanked me. I feel like I spoke from my heart - without all of society's "trappings." I think that is good. So why am I feeling so bad? I guess I am feeling bad because I wonder if I gave him the green light to dream and continue wanting to be in a band on tour. I don't want that. I believe so strongly that an education helps us to better understand the world and our place in it, that education is a must.

Reflecting now on that last paragraph, there are many things that make me cringe. But what stands out to me most is that because what I wanted was so important, I questioned whether I should have given our son the green light *to dream.* Somehow that is both humbling and frightening. Yes, my son was young and needed my guidance. But guiding is much different than mandating, and my Martha likes to mandate because my Martha thinks she knows what is best for everyone.

I have come to realize that as the mother of my children, I certainly had something to do with their creation, but I am not their Creator - and they cannot be whatever I want them to be. They must walk their own journey, the journey that God calls them to walk. On the other hand, God calls me, as their mother, to guide them. So for me, and I suppose for most parents, the most difficult questions in raising children have to do with negotiating that very fine line between setting boundaries and giving freedom. The dance to incorporate Mary's contemplation of God into Martha's parental expectations (or vice versa) is a very difficult dance indeed. Too much of Martha and I want to totally control my children; too much of Mary and I am willing to totally abdicate to my children. Finding the balance somewhere in between is both the joy and the nightmare of parenting.

What I have learned, however, is that when I place all of my "doing" within the greater context of God's presence and love, *I change the way I do what I do.* I do it with much more love, with a greater spirit of community, and with less earthly expectation. I do it in a way that gives due respect to both Martha and Mary and ultimately gives due respect to everyone involved. I *know* that at a prior time in my life I would not have been able to say to our son what I said that day. Incorporating Mary into my Martha changed me. Reflection changed my focus from me to our son. My inflexible attitude of "I know best" changed to a flexible and more open attitude, one much more conducive to the Holy Spirit's movement, one that for our family on that given day was what our son needed from me and what our relationship needed in general. To better understand myself and my son, I needed to move into that space between us. And that space required my willingness to change.

When our son was a teenager, I thought that I knew so much about what was best for him. God has taught me many lessons, however. I have learned that with prayer and self-reflection, I can more easily leave the certainty of single-mindedness and speak instead from the gray uncertainty of possibility. I have also learned that many different roads will take us to our destinations, and there is never a need for any two of those roads to be exactly the same. Our son did go to college directly from high school. How fitting it was that in his first year, in the room across the hall, lived a wonderful young man of faith who spent school breaks trying to improve the lives of the poor, a young man who quickly became one of our son's best friends, a young man who toured with a band his first year after high school.

* * *

I thought that the wisdom I had garnered during the process of raising our first-born would make raising our second-born much easier. In part, it did, but raising my daughter was to move me to a new kind of understanding.

I am a woman of words. I write, speak, journal, and process problems through words. They are, for me, a pathway to the unity I so desperately seek between my thoughts and my emotions. Words help bring me to a place of order, but I was soon to learn that, for some, words can be the source of great frustration. One evening our daughter was working on a junior high science fair project. She was not happy about how it was coming together; she was very tired and frustrated and began to cry. The hour was late, so with my words of analysis, I suggested that perhaps she should go to sleep and work on it the next day. Crying more, her reply was, "I can't. I have too much to do!" So I suggested that she wash her face, pull herself together, and work more that night. Crying even more, she replied, "I can't. I am too tired!" So, with my words of not only analysis, but also expedience, I stated the obvious: Crying doesn't help. It doesn't get you anywhere, which only elicited crying in crescendo fashion. Clearly, I had only succeeded in making my daughter more miserable, so I asked my husband to see what he could do. Five minutes later, I walked into her room and found her lying calmly on the bed while my husband rubbed her back. Soon, she was asleep. The next morning I asked her what her dad had done that I hadn't, and she responded, *"He didn't talk!"*

My spiritual director says that my daughter has called me to silence, and indeed she has. Perhaps I was finally beginning to understand that fact when I wrote this journal entry:

She doesn't need my rationality. She needs my emotional support. She goes where she gets quiet, emotional support. Without that realization, I can be a very loud gong.

Now, when I want to say something to my daughter, I ask myself these questions: Do I want to say this because it will make *me* feel better? Or do I want to say it because, as her mother, I think she needs to hear it? If it is the former, I remain quiet. If it is the latter, I speak it. More often than not, I remain quiet. This call to silence has been another lesson in moving myself out of the way so that the needs of others can be addressed. Difficult? For me, absolutely yes.

That space "in between" always is. Our priest has often reminded us, however, that Joseph speaks no words in the Bible - but is far from silent. A lesson, no doubt, which demands my reflection.

* * *

I learned about trusting and letting go in another interesting experience when our son was thinking about becoming engaged. So excited about that possibility, our now teenaged daughter often wondered about the details of the engagement proposal and eagerly anticipated the event. I knew it would mean so much to her if her brother would include her in his plans, and I very much wanted to ask him to do just that. But as much as I wanted to act and ensure that my daughter would have this gift, I also knew that there was one very significant reason that I could not orchestrate it: the gift was not mine to give. My interference would deprive our son of the opportunity to authentically give it and would also deny our daughter of the opportunity to meaningfully receive it. So I stayed quiet, knowing, of course, that the gift might not be given at all.

Months passed and then one night we received a phone call from our son and future daughter-in-law announcing their engagement. We were elated. Our daughter was not home, so I said that I would ask her to return the call and, in the meantime, would not tell her the news. Later that evening, when our daughter made the call, I heard her excitedly say, "You did?!" Then she turned to me and said, "I already knew."

My heart, so full of joy, felt like it would explode. Love was expressed and relationship made closer, all because I did not do what I very much wanted to do, all because desired action tempered with contemplation once again brought me to a space where my family could flourish.

* * *

Being most fully human requires that I inhabit the space "in between" the opposites, away from the one-dimensional extreme to a place where a wider understanding is possible and where diversity can exist within the common ground of sameness. Love is the catalyst for this journey, and change is the result. God's powerful love has changed me. It has created movement notwithstanding my stubbornness; it has changed my way of seeing notwithstanding my obstinance; and it has brought me to a place of togetherness notwithstanding my selfishness. The movement that required me to embrace both my head and my heart is the same movement that nudged me, sometimes shoved me, into a place somewhere between many other opposites. In that "in between" space, I would come to better understand myself, my neighbor, and my God, and I would come to discover a space that nourishes understanding, relationship, peace, and unity.

Continuously challenged by Jesus' commandment, I struggle to be my best self for the sake of all of us. I struggle to embrace the process of change that requires acknowledgment of my flawed and broken humanity, that requires desire to become better, and that requires overcoming my own illusion of perfection which manifests itself in the notion that I know - and others do not. But when I embrace the hard work of relationships, I find fertile ground for joyful possibilities exactly at the point where the struggle for human excellence is most clearly evident: when I try to unify the contrasts in my life. It is a struggle because it requires that I love even when I am angry or hurt, that I become the student when I would much rather be the teacher, that I protect my family members while encouraging them to grow and become the unique individuals they were called to be. Finding the right place between self-care and self-sacrifice, between possessing and letting go, between what is and what can be is a tall order, even within a relationship of love, but the possibilities of change are much more liberating than the certainties of arrogance.

For people like me who want certainty and control, Martha together with Mary place us exactly where we do not want to be: in uncertain territory with limited control. But in that frightening "in between" where change is fostered, the surprising end is peace - internally and with others. It seems that when I lower myself from a god-like know-it-all to a human being with both gifts and faults, I also elevate others from foolish human beings to respectable human beings. Honesty about who I am makes me human, not a god, and that fact alone gives life to my relationships.

CHAPTER EIGHT

To the "In Between" Through Fiction

My one-sided way of thinking was again challenged during the first semester of my master's program. Notwithstanding my undergraduate English degree, during my legal career I had limited my reading to nonfiction: legal cases, legal commentary, legal analysis, books about ethics, books on religion, everything nonfiction. I had reached the conclusion that I could learn more from nonfiction than fiction and more from the ancients than from my contemporaries.

When signing up for the one class that I would take that semester, I discovered there was only one class that fit my schedule, and it was *Contemporary Fiction*. I did not want to take it. What could I possibly learn? But I wanted to begin my studies, and this was the only class that I *could* take. I had a gnawing suspicion that I *should* take it, so I did. The course was the study of one South African author, J. M. Coetzee; we would read seven of his novels.

I got off to a rocky start. The violence was more than I could handle. I dotted the margins with exclamation points where I was appalled by what I was reading. At one point, I even wrote "This is ridiculous!" in the margin. So in class one day, when the professor asked if there might be a reason for a reader to return the book, I had no trouble responding. "I would give this book back in a minute," I said. "I would never have chosen to read it. I don't want to know about the details of killing; it is way too violent for me." In response, the professor very calmly suggested that I should consider whether I belonged in the class. He tried to explain how my viewpoint might be blinding me to something hidden but important. It was time for class to end, so he concluded with the remark that we would begin the next class "with Susan reading aloud." I stayed afterwards to talk to him about the class, its meaning, its importance. He disclosed that the class was really one about ethics and suggested that I read ahead to a book that was less violent so that I could assess whether or not I wanted to continue studying these works.

I stayed. As the days and weeks passed, I began to discover that Coetzee was very adept at creating characters who wanted to do the right thing but did not know how, because they did not know or understand the people around them. I watched the behavior of characters who were "in" and the behavior of characters who were "out." I became more cognizant of the horrific effects of arrogance and presumption and all their complexities. At the end of the semester, I cried during my final presentation because I had been so moved by the literature.

Reading about characters who described boundaries with such confident precision - and reading about characters for whom that confident precision was misplaced - propelled me to long for some place "in between" where there could be understanding. I felt like I could understand the characters, but they could not understand each other. I wanted to help break down the barriers. I wanted them to know each other as the people they were, not as people defined by others' perceptions of them. My heart began to open as worldly materiality, found in things such as status and power, fueled the inaccurate presumptions that accompany labeling. My intellect began to recognize the many ways in which broad generalizations served to create and disseminate false information. I found myself moving from intellectual antipathy regarding labeling to emotional commitment against it. There is something much more personal and urgent about that message. It is the difference between recognizing that a problem exists and being "all in" to do something about it.

By encountering the violence which I hated, I had the opportunity to reflect on human behavior, mine and others. Through those readings, I not only knew intellectually that violence was wrong, which I knew before I took the class, I also felt it in my heart. I yearned even more robustly for understanding, for a place away from arrogant assumptions and quiet suffering, for a middle ground where all can be respected, worthy, and dignified, for a pathway forged by trust, understanding, and love rather than suspicion, presumption, and hatred. It was, once again, a change from intellect only to a place where intellect and heart unite to create a different way of seeing. Intellect can observe the suffering but cannot feel it. Intellect can analyze the data but cannot quantify the impact of the exception. Heart can take us into the suffering and can grant mercy and forgiveness when it would make no intellectual sense to do so. While intellect is on alert to the dangers of difference, heart finds its way toward sameness.

During my studies, emotional experience softened the boundaries created by my intellect. Once again, I was learning that intellectual knowledge, valuable in so many areas of our lives, can be sterile with regard to how we see each other and how we treat each other. The last paragraph of my final paper summed up the experience:

"Awakening. Otherness. Moral compass. Bafflement. Examination of characters. Examination of self. Border blurring. Border crossing. An evolving, moving event. Movement toward a better world. Hope. Justice. Who would have ever imagined that such thought-provoking experiences could all radiate from what I considered a minor, insubstantial, and vacuous art form known as fiction? What a delightful discovery . . . ."

Coetzee's characters who were "other," were often moved to silence, a silence that reflected the impossibility of understanding difference, the impossibility of interpreting others in any way other than through our own lens. In *Waiting for the Barbarians*, a revealing title in and of itself, Coetzee treats the subject of colonial oppression so realistically that the reader cannot help but question and explore his/her own prejudices and behaviors. The magistrate has sexual relations with the "barbarian girl" but never knows her; he studies her but never understands her; he uses her in an attempt to quell his own shame but nevertheless fails to quiet his inner conscience. He wants so much to help her, yet he never discovers what hurts her.[9]

How difficult it is to tap the core of our commonality when appearance, intelligence, and occupation are only a few of the many ways that humans rank each other. How does anyone successfully navigate the seas of illusion, confusion, and classification in order to discover the truth? How is one to include the marginalized, the silenced? How is one to know racial or class authenticity or any other type of authenticity? Perhaps the polarity of another can never be truly understood, but a desire to understand at least holds the potential for movement *toward* the other. And movement toward another can create space that houses a new possibility. Father Greg Boyle, a priest who works with gang members in Los Angeles, beautifully describes the new possibility that he seeks: ". . .

---

9   See Coetzee, J.M. (1982). *Waiting for the Barbarians.* Penguin Books.

A compassion that can stand in awe at what the poor have to carry rather than stand in judgment at how they carry it."[10] Awe rather than judgment. What a lovely possibility.

---

10 Boyle, G. (2010). *Tattoos on the Heart*. Free Press. p. 67.

CHAPTER NINE

Love's Movement to the "In Between" Through Anxiety

When our daughter was nine years old and in the fourth grade, she was diagnosed with an anxiety disorder. Stepping into school every morning became a monumental endeavor. The professionals (including a child psychologist friend of ours) all said the same thing: *she had to go to school.* I begged for explanations; I stayed up until all hours of the morning learning all I could about anxiety; I talked to anyone and everyone I thought might give me some direction. I cried - a lot. What I was being told to do went against every maternal instinct that I had, and I thought I wouldn't be able to stand it. How could we continue to force her to go to school? All I wanted to do was bring her home and homeschool her. *Why* couldn't I do that? Our friend confirmed the reasons: if I homeschooled our daughter, she would learn that whenever she was afraid, she could stay home or go home, and her world would get very small. Additionally, she would be denied the opportunity to discover the inner strength that would ultimately get her through.

Our daughter's pleas to not make her go to school still resound in my ears all these years later and can still bring me to tears. All I ever knew about loving a child was not being evidenced one iota in the scenario that the professionals around me were constructing. Permeating my journal are entries asking God to help me know what was best for our daughter, pleading with God to give us strength, begging God to please take this illness away from her. My journal is filled with my angst, and worse, with the angst of knowing that if I felt this bad, how in the world must she feel? We were on a path that I had never traveled and my instincts were telling me that the map I was given was taking me in the wrong direction. How could I possibly agree? This was my *daughter.*

We asked questions. We attended meetings in order to devise what we hoped would be workable plans. I tried to explain these plans to my beautiful, nine-year old child who was doing the very best she could to endure what I could only imagine . . . but every plan included the assumption that she would walk into her classroom at a particular time every morning - so every plan was fraught with much difficulty for her.

My heart didn't just ache; it bled. The nights were unbearable, and the days were worse. The boundaries were so unclear for all of us. And when she began to act out, we were told that we *must* maintain the boundaries we had always set for our children, that doing so was necessary to lessen the confusion that swirled around us all. So we stood very firm in our expectations - adding daggers to my already bleeding heart. It was three months of crisis, turmoil, and deep, penetrating heartache.

But with God's grace, we all endured. That year, and in the years that followed, we learned about challenging our one-sided thoughts and our one-sided emotions. Our daughter learned to challenge her fear and turn her experience into one of strength. Every day, she had to engage in the practice of doing the opposite of what her fear directed her to do. And ultimately, we were able to find a way for both of us to walk *through.*

Not surprisingly, it was in the middle place once again. Whenever our daughter had a difficult time getting to school in the morning, I would walk into the building with her and sit in a non-classroom space. If she needed to sit with me, she could. If she didn't need to, she would go to class. I would stay until she was comfortable. That was the middle ground we forged. It worked for us because I did not have other small children at home and because by then I had left the practice of law and was back in school. The reading and writing I needed to do could be done from the room in which I sat.

By giving our daughter control over when she went into her classroom on any given morning, we no longer had to force her to go to school. By being there to provide comfort to her, I no longer felt compelled to take her home. We moved toward her, she was able to move toward us, and the possibility of loving movement from self to other became very real. The extremes were giving way to a middle. Force and total abdication were a thing of the past, and our daughter was now facing her fears within a framework of love.

But that doesn't mean that middle space was easy. One very difficult morning, I was struggling to find a way through the opposites. I was walking the fine line between comforting and pushing. And I was getting frustrated - *with her.* My daughter sensed it, and in her youthful wisdom, calmly and lovingly said, "If you understood, you wouldn't be frustrated." I did not understand that sentence then, but now I realize what a wonderfully true statement it is. At that time, I expected her to find the strength and the will to do what she needed to do. I did not understand her struggle because I looked at her fear rationally, saw no basis for it, and thought it should be easily quieted. I did not understand the strength of that fear. I did not understand anxiety *disorder.* All I thought about was how I overcame my *normal* anxiety. I did not realize how much will and determination she was exercising simply by doing what she *was* doing: *trying very hard to do the right thing.* She was not being obstinate; she had an illness and was doing the very best she could. And what she needed from me was understanding and support - not labels, derision, or frustration - because they simply fueled more misunderstanding. My daughter was right: If I understood, I would not have been frustrated.

I realize now that my frustration probably stemmed, at least in part, from the fact that I was placed in that very difficult middle spot where what I had to do seemed so, so incredibly hard. I wanted to do nothing but comfort, but I also needed to push. How much and to what extent were simply a matter of trial and error. Too much comfort would stifle her because she desperately wanted to cling to that comfort. Too little comfort would also stifle her because it didn't provide the support she needed to fuel the courage within her. In my journal, I wrote my prayer:

Help me, God, please, to know when to hug, when to push, when to praise, when to encourage, when to draw the line, when to negotiate its movement. I love her so much. Help me to help her - in a way that is best for her - not me. I must do what I am pushing her to do: Deal with it, don't escape from it, make the hard choices and do the difficult things. I will do the best I can, God, but I really need you to guide me. With you, I can do anything I need to do. Help me to hear you; help me to always reflect your love.

Strength waxes and wanes for all of us, but our family has learned that over time if we face something that is difficult, it becomes a tiny bit easier to face the next time, and the next time, and the next time, for *all* of us, with or without an anxiety disorder. We gradually internalize the other voice, and a possibility becomes a reality. As Aristotle said, the *act* of doing is what makes the doing possible: Playing the piano provides the skills for being a piano player; building provides the skills for being a builder; being brave provides the skills necessary to be brave.[11] Our call to growth, when faced and embraced, enables joyful possibility to become a reality.

Our daughter has taught me much about courage and fortitude. She has taught me that we must step into that unknown and do what needs to be done to move us to the good. She has taught me that although it is difficult to find and travel a middle path, love will always light the way through our challenges, trials, and suffering. Praying and asking for God's guidance, I wrote in my journal:

Do I make it more difficult than it is? Just love. Don't worry about anything else. Just love.

In another day of quiet prayer in the chapel, I wrote:

"I have prayed every day for my daughter's healing. Maybe I should focus on my own healing - my own journey to quietness. Maybe if I make myself a better person, she will be better."

We have the power to transform each other, but to effectively do so, we must first transform ourselves. And in that transformation lies an abundance of joyful possibilities.

I used to tell my daughter that though her anxiety was difficult, the difficulties would mold her to do the work she is called to do in her life. I can now see that all of those experiences in her very young life began the process of her empowerment, a process which has shaped the person she has become. Those three months in fourth grade were the beginning of a process in which she discovered her strength and turned her helplessness into the power of self advocacy.

---

11 Aristotle. (2004) *The Nicomachean Ethics.* (Thomson, J.A.K., Trans.). Penguin Books.

Her experiences in grade school and the years that followed were the beginning of her process of self-knowledge. And over these many years, I have watched her cross turn into a gift. When working with children, she has an uncanny ability to connect with them *all*; she recognizes their individuality: their gifts, challenges, needs, and differences. And remembering the helplessness of her own elementary school experience has enabled her to embrace them with a much wider band of understanding.

At Christmas of our daughter's junior year of college, she gave me one of the most meaningful gifts I have ever received: a wall hanging in her own handwriting with this saying from Keion Jackson:[12]

Mama looked into
me and saw something
worth believing in,
long before I believed
in myself.

"Mama," the name she called me as a child, evoked such a feeling of personal closeness within me, and the remaining words lifted my heart as they joyfully affirmed the power of a mother's love.

* * *

12 *We Heart Mom: Mother's Day Stories From Hallmark Writers.* (2015, May 8). ThinkMakeShareBlog. Retrieved June 2020, from https://www.thinkmakeshareblog. com/mothers-day-stories/

Through my daughter, I was beginning to learn about Martha and Mary from the vantage point of suffering. Although it took much time and effort on all of our parts, I ultimately learned I was powerless to take her illness away, but I could nonetheless support her in a way that was useful. Our daughter ultimately learned that meeting the illness head on, understanding it and herself, and assuming responsibility for her own life were the roles cast to her. Our views of ourselves changed, but there is no doubt that this process moved both of us from our comfortable extreme to a place where we did not want to be.

At some time or another all of us land on that kind of path, a path we do not want to travel. It may be the path of illness; it may be the path of a broken relationship; it may be our own path or the path of someone we love so much that we wish it were our own path. Whatever it is, we have no power to change it. We are in the midst of a dark, unfamiliar, and frightening course. The suffering stabs us by day and gnaws at us by night. The gravity of the challenge sometimes seems too heavy to bear. A Martha like me wants to *do* something. A Martha like me wants to *fix it*. And yet a Martha like me has no choice but to acknowledge that she is powerless. Now, my Martha is weak, but my Mary is strong. Mary will sit at the feet of Jesus and listen to him - and his words will echo a bit differently in Martha's ears: "Martha, Martha, you are anxious and worried about many things. There is need of only one thing. Mary has chosen the better part, and it will not be taken from her." Now, far from making my Martha angry, these words bring her great peace and comfort. Now, the "in between" houses another option: sitting at the feet of Jesus, listening, trusting, and being strengthened in love.

CHAPTER TEN

The "In Between" and Transformation

Nearly two decades ago, I embarked on a journey whose shape I could not envision, a journey that moved me toward a place in the middle where I could experience love in a more generous and magnificent form. That journey toward the middle has sometimes reminded me of playing "monkey in the middle" as a child. I never wanted to be in the middle; I don't think anyone did. The middle was hard. The two people on the ends had control of the ball, and the person in the middle had to try to take it from them. Those on the ends could throw it very high over the head and out of the reach of the middle person who, in order to get to the ball, had to jump higher, run faster, and be on alert for any mistake the others might make. It took a great deal more energy to be the monkey in the middle than it did to be on either end because the middle person had to cover all the space *in between* the two ends. But there is, nonetheless, something very important about that middle: I can be in the middle *and still embrace the endpoint* - but I cannot remain at the endpoint and also embrace what is in between, and that fact alone makes the in between, the middle, a much wider path for understanding.

For me, prayer and honest self-reflection are good starting points to an "in between" space. They give me a broader and more realistic vision of myself and of others. That broader vision fosters humility, which opens the door to acceptance of the fact that *I just may not be the only person in the world to whom God has entrusted wisdom.*

(Imagine that . . . .) And that discovery enables me to hear diverse voices which help me see differently, think differently, embrace new possibilities, and gradually begin to *change*.

* * *

But transformation makes me vulnerable and unsettled and is not an easy process. Without change, however, there is no possibility of *becoming*, of improving, in whatever manner is necessary for me to be a more loving human being. Without change, who I am today is who I will be at the instant of my death. Without change, in troubled relationships it will always be one of us against another of us until power or brute force wins out. But peaceful coexistence among human beings is a prerequisite for the *existence* of human beings, so I have concluded that if finding common ground in the space between us requires some change on my part, then surely change is the journey on which I must embark.

But that new picture, necessary as it is, is not easy to accept. My "hardness of heart" (Mark 3:5) resists movement from rule to relationship. It was no different during the time of Jesus when his new world order emphasized people rather than ritual and tradition. His curing of a crippled woman on the sabbath was unacceptable to the indignant synagogue leader who told the crowd to come for healing on the six days when work should be done, not on the sabbath (Luke 13:12-14). When truth is not easy to accept, hardness of heart easily turns away from it.

Similarly, after the blind man was healed, the Pharisees asked many questions to try to understand what had happened. Finally, the blind man said, "It is unheard of that anyone ever opened the eyes of a person born blind. If this man were not from God, he would not be able to do anything" (John 9:32-33). With that, the indignation of the Pharisees got the best of them, and their task shifted: No longer were they concerned about discovering the truth of what happened. They were now concerned only with proving their superiority as they threw the blind man out, saying, "You were born totally in sin, and are you trying to teach us?" (John 9:34). How easy it is to forget truth in order to protect a fragile ego . . . .

And King Herod finds himself in a similar situation. Desiring to reward his daughter for performing a dance that delighted him and his banquet guests, he offered to grant her whatever she asked. When the girl, at the request of her mother, asked for the head of John the Baptist, Herod, although distressed, ordered the beheading to protect his reputation with the guests (Mark 6:22-28). Movement from rewarding a daughter to satisfying a personal need was quick and easy.

But rather than a quick and easy turn from the truth, transformation of self requires an embrace of the truth - and must begin with a self that is strong enough to defer, a confidence that is sturdy enough to be mistaken, and a love that is true enough to embrace another.

Many would argue that such a process is wrong because it means giving up our principles or values. But personal transformation does not mean we must relinquish our values. It simply means we must accept the opportunity to look at the situation in a broader context. When I wanted to tell my son he had to go to college and could not go on tour with a band, I was clinging to two values: that he would receive a higher education and that he would make healthy and moral choices with his life. Those values never changed. But my transformation helped me to see *what I brought to those values*: a belief that higher education had to begin directly after high school, my own generalizations and prejudices about teenage bands, and all the accompanying fears and "what ifs." Once I realized how I was clouding the situation, and once I saw my son realistically and outside my own fears, I could take note of the fact that he was already embodying the values that I wanted for him. He was a terrific student, and he had shown me many times over that he knew how to make healthy and moral choices. Change never altered my values; it only softened the hardness of my heart and moved me from an impediment to a more understanding guide.

In his book, *The Beatitudes: Soundings in Christian Tradition,* Simon Tugwell writes about the necessity of being open to a broader and less arrogant way of thinking and seeing:

> "The temptation, in any kind of controversy, is to harden our own position and emphasize its distance from the position of our opponents, and there is no doubt that Christians have often in fact argued this way. But the Church as a whole can never rest content with such a procedure . . . Any serious and useful undertaking produces a crop of different opinions and schools of thought, and it is from a careful scrutiny of all of them that man becomes genuinely wise . . . We must be prepared to insist on what we see to be true and to remind people of the evidence of our contentions . . . but we must not do this arrogantly, as if we were in full possession of the entire truth. We must hold on to what we see to be true, or even what we consider to be the most probable, as our contribution to the eventual discovery of all truth. But we must be fully prepared to find that such eventual discovery puts our little bit of truth in a light very different from that in which we ourselves saw it."[13]

---

13 Tugwell, S. (1980). *The Beatitudes: Soundings in Christian Traditions.* Templegate Publishers. pp. 119-120.

Love is the path to this broader understanding. When it is not easy to love, I remind myself that Jesus' mandate to love has no qualifiers. He did not say to love God only when life is comfortable or I get what I want. He did not say to love my neighbor only when he/she agrees with me. And he did not say to love myself only if and when I can meet the expectations of the material world around me. He said that I must *love*. Period.

Where there is difference, there is also the potential for creative newness and unlimited, even unimagined, possibility; I only have to diligently seek it. And when I do, understanding, connection, dignity, and respect just may win out over arrogance, oppression, and violent force. And Jesus' mandate to love God and neighbor as self just may be realized.

I am not advocating that the middle, the "in between," is always the right place to be. That too would be an extreme. Aristotle was clear: Sometimes the mean is inapplicable. A little bit of envy is still envy; a little bit of murder is still murder.[14] But I have learned that the absolutes are fewer than I had originally thought - and in the space that contains that which binds us together as humans, there is room for inner change that comes about when, through God's graces, the artificial, superficial, and irrelevant begin to fall away.

What I *am* advocating is that we begin to desire truth, begin to open our minds to what we may not know, begin to find our way to and through that messy middle where our common humanity takes precedence over our individual rightness. For this to happen, human beings must be given dignity and respect *and* human beings must exercise the necessary concomitant responsibility.

---

14 Aristotle. (2004) *The Nicomachean Ethics*. (Thomson, J.A.K., Trans.). Penguin Books.

As humans we do not have the power to eradicate all that is bad, hurtful, or hateful in our world, but that does not mean we are helpless. Full power to eradicate and no power at all are the two extremes. Somewhere in between is the place where we must find our way to a more humane, peaceful, and loving world. If we are going to attempt to walk *through* the issues that divide us, and I believe we must, then trying to find our way to the "in between" through love may at least bring us to the same table and make discourse possible.

PART III:
WHO WE ARE
AS HUMAN BEINGS

In God's image and good.
Divinity and humanity united.
Infinite joyful possibilities unleashed.

CHAPTER ELEVEN

Reflection on the First Chapters of Genesis

Contrasts within our human nature are part of our human reality. We have the capacity to think and feel, to protect self and make room for others, to be in the present but remember the past and imagine the future. The opposites tug at us, and life imposes on us the task of finding a path *through*.

But when we walk through difference, our actions are often guided by hurt, anger, ego, control, status, or some other worldly value - and these often obstruct our views and preclude us from moving to a more objective and moderate "in between." Although humans cannot be perfect, the human/divine contrast provides significance to our humanity, provides a perfection we can attempt to emulate, and provides God's graces for the journey. It is the mystery at the heart of our humanity.

The first three chapters of Genesis speak to the essence of our humanity.

(1) God created mankind:
   * "God created man in his image . . ." (1:27).
   * " . . .[T]he Lord God formed man out of the clay of the ground and blew into his nostrils the breath of life, and so man became a living being" (2:7).
   * "God looked at everything he had made, and he found it very good" (1:31).

We are created in God's image and we are good, notwithstanding that we are formed from the material of the ground.

(2) God created trees in the Garden of Eden and prohibited eating from one of them:

* "Out of the ground the Lord God made various trees grow that were delightful to look at and good for food, with the tree of life in the middle of the garden and the tree of the knowledge of good and bad" (2:9).

* "The Lord God gave man this order: 'You are free to eat from any of the trees of the garden except the tree of knowledge of good and bad. From that tree you shall not eat; the moment you eat from it you are surely doomed to die'" (2:16-17).

We are created in God's image and we are good, notwithstanding that we have the freedom to do what God forbids us to do.

(3) Temptation lurked:

* "But the serpent said to the woman: 'You certainly will not die! No, God knows well that the moment you eat of it your eyes will be opened and you will be like gods who know what is good and what is bad'" (3:4-5).

We are created in God's image and we are good, notwithstanding the allure of temptation.

(4) Adam and Eve ate the forbidden fruit:

* "The woman saw that the tree was good for food, pleasing to the eyes, and desirable for gaining wisdom. So she took some of its fruit and ate it; and she also gave some to her husband, who was with her, and he ate it. Then the eyes of both of them were opened, and they realized that they were naked; so they sewed fig leaves together and made loincloths for themselves" (3:6-7).

We are created in God's image and we are good, notwithstanding that sometimes we yield to temptation.

We are created in God's image and good. *That* is who we are as human beings. And goodness has no qualifiers. Genesis doesn't say that we are good only if we do not exercise our freedom; on the contrary, we are good, *and* we have freedom. The human being of Genesis must embrace numerous conflicting inner forces: humanity/divinity, materiality/spirituality, freedom/responsibility, desire/restraint, appearance/reality, falsity/truth, life/death. The push-and-pull between those forces and the push-and-pull between the Creator and the created are necessary consequences of a humanity that is good, created in God's image, and free to make choices. There is nothing simple about that fact. But if goodness and being made in God's image are the first and primary characteristics of our humanity, then everything else about being human, including all the conflicting forces within us, will find grounding in that foundational core of goodness.

Traditionally, the story of Adam and Eve represents mankind's fall away from God. But in their book, *Wrestling with Angels*, Naomi Rosenblatt and Joshua Horwitz suggest that mortality was the destiny of Adam and Eve[15] and that their going forth from the Garden of Eden represents, rather, the ". . . 'rise of man' as the first man and woman forge a covenant of love and interdependence dedicated to their mutual survival and growth."[16]

Perhaps both interpretations are true. Adam and Eve have separated from God, no doubt; they are banished from the Garden and rebuked by God. But I am greatly moved by the words that are nestled in between the rebuke and the banishment: "For the man and his wife the Lord God made leather garments with which he clothed them" (Gen 3:21). *God equips Adam and Eve with the necessary*

---

15 Rosenblatt, N., Horwitz, J. (1995). *Wrestling with Angels.* Delacorte Press. p. 48.
16 Rosenblatt, N., Horwitz, J. (1995). *Wrestling with Angels.* Delacorte Press. p. 44.

provisions to go forth outside of the Garden. Separation and "fall" bring with them strength to "rise" because God provides our humanity with what it needs. Although we may separate from him, God does not separate from us; our created human goodness is inextricably tied to our Creator's eternal goodness, and in that fact lies the joyful possibility that we can rise anew in God.

God makes "rising above" possible again in Chapter 4 when he speaks to Cain before he murders his brother Abel:

> "Why are you so resentful and crestfallen? If you do well, you can hold up your head; but if not, sin is a demon lurking at the door: his urge is toward you, yet you can be his master" (Gen 4:7).

We have the power to master the demons that are lurking at our door. Self/other, love/hate are additional conflicting forces which require us to assume the responsibility of discernment, the responsibility of harnessing the stabilizing and foundational goodness of our humanity to master the demons and achieve ". . . the tension which is constitutive for man: the *mean* which is being human."[17]   But employing that tension for the good is not easy, as C. S. Lewis observes:

> "Sometimes, Lord, one is tempted to say that if you wanted us to behave like the lilies of the field you might have given us an organization more like theirs. But that, I suppose, is just your grand experiment. Or no; not an experiment, for you have no need to find things out. Rather your grand enterprise. To make an organism which is also a spirit; to make that terrible oxymoron, a 'spiritual animal.' To take a poor primate, a beast with nerve-endings all over it, a creature with a stomach that wants to be filled, a breeding animal that wants its mate, and say, 'Now get on with it. Become a god.'"[18]

---

17 Kasper, W. (2011). *Jesus the Christ.* Continuum Books. p. 43.
18 Lewis, C.S. (1961). *A Grief Observed.* HarperCollins. p. 57.

CHAPTER TWELVE

God Continues to Provide Through Jesus

On this journey of "becoming," God has provided for his people throughout history - not only in the early chapters of Genesis but also throughout the Old Testament and again through the life of Jesus in the New Testament. Both divine and human, Jesus demonstrates how to allow our divine roots to provoke purifying growth toward God. Jesus' entire life testifies to the wonders of such a journey, but for me, some of the images that most poignantly capture this growth are those of yeast, cultivation, water, and light.

Yeast

In Luke 13:20-21, Jesus compares the kingdom of God to yeast: "It is like yeast that a woman took and mixed [in] with three measures of wheat flour until the whole batch of dough was leavened." Divine leaven is mixed with the earthly, and growth is stimulated. Like the bread dough that my parents placed in their bakery steam boxes to rise, so my life, situated amid God's presence and divine graces, wells up and expands as God intensifies my passion, magnifies the capacity of my head and heart, expands my vision, and increases my ability to love.

Cultivation

In John 15:1-4, Jesus says:

"I am the true vine, and my Father is the vine grower. He takes away every branch in me that does not bear fruit, and everyone that does he prunes so that it bears more fruit. You are already pruned because of the word that I spoke to you. Remain in me, as I remain in you. Just as a branch cannot bear fruit on its own unless it remains on the vine, so neither can you unless you remain in me."

And in Luke 8:15, Jesus says:

" . . .[A]s for the seed that fell on rich soil, they are the ones who, when they have heard the word, embrace it with a generous and good heart, and bear fruit through perseverance."

Jesus' words regarding planting seeds and bearing fruit remind me of time spent with my dad in his vegetable garden. His strong hands gingerly placed the seeds in the ground and then covered them with soil - not too heavy or packed down to inhibit growth, not too light or scant to insufficiently support growth, just a perfect balance of what was necessary to nurture emerging life. And when weeding the garden, my dad's hands were at once both scythe and earnest protector, matter-of-factly discarding the unnecessary while caressing the essential. Even when the weeds were intertwined with the fruit-bearing plant, he had an uncanny ability to remove the weed without disturbing the integrity of the plant, and he seemed to do it in one easy motion.

My dad's actions help me understand Jesus' message. If I follow Jesus' word, God will prune my life. The nonproductive will fall away, and the fruitful will be fortified. Jesus' word, God's pruning, and my *becoming* will intertwine in a beautiful process of growth. And that process of growth will strengthen my core, shape my movement, and empower me to embrace goodness and charity as I persevere on this journey of life. My responsibility is simply to stay connected to my Creator. If I do, just as the seed, the vine, and the bread dough are all nurtured to their fullest potential, so God will cultivate me so that each step in the process of becoming yields new and emerging life.

Water

If God nourishes me to life, then certainly water is a fitting image. Psalm 42:2-3 reads: "As the deer longs for streams of water, so my soul longs for you, O God. My being thirsts for God, the living God." In the New Testament, in John 7:38, Jesus says: "Whoever believes in me . . . '[r]ivers of living water will flow from within him.'" And in John 4:13-14: " . . . The water I shall give will become in him a spring of water welling up to eternal life." I love that these images of water are not images of contained lakes but rather images of energetic, active, and freely flowing rivers and streams. Jesus provides what we need *to live.* New Testament images of life-giving water are also images of purity and abundant yield:

> "Then the angel showed me the river of life-giving water, sparkling like crystal, flowing from the throne of God and of the Lamb down the middle of the street. On either side of the river grew the tree of life that produces fruit twelve times a year, once each month . . . " (Rev 22:1-2) .

The nourishment that Jesus provides is pure and radiant and satisfies our needs over and over again. Jesus, both human and divine - water, both physical and spiritual nourishment.

Light

Jesus also provides when he says: "I am the light of the world. Whoever follows me will not walk in darkness, but will have the light of life" (John 8:12). He guides us through our complex nature by illuminating the path, providing increased vision, orienting us in our surroundings, and leading us to the glory of God. And divine light is liberating. The night the angel freed Peter from imprisonment, "a light shone in the cell" (Acts 12:7). And Saul's conversion from Christian persecutor to Christian advocate began when "a light from the sky suddenly flashed around him" (Acts 9:3). Divine light carries with it the possibility of both physical and spiritual freedom. But that is not all. Jesus says that the light of God is not only "out there" to be embraced; the light of God also shines within us:

> "You are the light of the world. A city set on a mountain cannot be hidden. Nor do they light a lamp and then put it under a bushel basket; it is set on a lamp stand, where it gives light to all in the house. Just so, your light must shine before others, that they may see your good deeds and glorify your heavenly Father" (Matt 5:14-16).

Human beings created in the image of God *are made to shine,* made to embrace, reflect, and emit the luminosity of the divine. In mystifyingly boundless ways, complex and imperfect human beings are made to move toward the pure light of God in the powerful activity of *becoming.* Connecting with the leaven of God's kingdom fosters our growth, nourishes our life, quenches our thirst, and provides us with the illumination necessary to shine. Connecting to this pure and perfect goodness, whose graces are both compelling and inexplicable, is the antidote to our imperfect and limited humanity.

* * *

Connecting to this pure and perfect goodness is our source of contentment and when we lose that connection, we suffer. Rev. Dr. Martin Luther King, Jr. says that mankind is ". . . made for the stars, created for the everlasting, born for eternity . . . crowned with glory and honor, and so long as he lives on the low level he will be frustrated, disillusioned, and bewildered."[19] I have experienced that frustration and disillusionment in my most difficult relationships. No matter how hard I tried, I could not move past the hurt I felt. I would do it for a while, but then the other person's word or action would bring that hurt and my accompanying emotions to the foreground once again. When I was angry, in my mind I would smugly list the ways I had been treated unjustly. Then, trying to regain my bearings, I would pray and ask God for help. Usually, I vacillated between prayer and self-righteous recitation until an exit from the cycle finally appeared.

But at the point of exit, prayer had changed the anger into something less threatening and more understanding. Aggression, hate, and selfishness seemed to move out of the way to make room for God's love. Jesus' word, God's pruning, and the process of becoming - all made real. Being "made for the stars" seemed a possibility once again. But it was only on a journey with God that my eyes began to open, my heart began to change, and benevolence and affection began to replace my anger. Father Boyle says, "Sooner or later, we all discover that kindness is the only strength there is."[20] Kindness *is* our strength - because authentic kindness reflects the goodness of

---

19 King, M.L. (1988). *The Measure of a Man.* Fortress Press. p. 26.
20 Boyle, G. (2010). *Tattoos on the Heart.* Free Press. p. 124.

the giver, considers the needs of the receiver, and depends on the proposition that *both* are "made for the stars" and worthy. Kindness is a divine vehicle for *becoming.*

CHAPTER THIRTEEN

Human Worth

Human beings are inherently worthy because we are created by God in his image - and cared for by God as he provides all that we need. Even all the hairs on our heads have been counted (Luke 12:7). But we do not always accept that inherent worth. Not content with who we are, we look for worth elsewhere, often by comparing ourselves to others. We think we are able to find out who *we* are by looking at who *others* are. Yet as philosopher Soren Kierkegaard observes:

> " . . . from 'the others', naturally, one properly only learns to know what the others are - it is in this way the world would beguile a man from being himself. 'The others', in turn, do not know at all what they themselves are, but only what the others are."[21]

There are significant consequences to trying to discover our human worth by comparing ourselves to others. First and foremost, our worth is made conditional; it exists *only if* we measure up. And the requirements for measuring up lie in the material world, so they may be unattainable: we may never look like, or have the same skills as, the ones whose standards we embrace. Additionally, worth is made elusive and fleeting because even if we do measure up, we do so only until the standard for measuring up changes or until someone else with "more" comes along. When we compare ourselves to others,

---

21 Kierkegaard, S. (1971). *Christian Discourses, etc.* (Lowrie, W., Trans.). Princeton University Press. p. 43.

we are never good enough, and we can never be confident in who we are. Consequently, movement forward is stagnated by confusion, disorientation, powerlessness, and despair.

Comparing ourselves to others skews our vision of ourselves. Perhaps that is the reason the first of the Ten Commandments directs that we shall have no other gods besides the Lord. When we compare ourselves to others, instead of trying to reflect God in whose image we are made, we try to reflect other human beings, as though we were made in their image. Worshipping the earthly instead of our God, we engage in idolatry (See Col 3:5). But Jesus tells us that being worthy simply requires that we worship God: that we accept God's invitation (see Matt 22:1-9), that we acknowledge our unworthiness and have faith in God's power of restoration (see Matt 8:5-13), that we take up our cross, follow Jesus, and place God above all that is loved in this world (see Matt 10:37-38).

When human worth is tied to God, worth is *given*, not earned, worth is consistent and immutable, and we are more than "good enough." When our worth is tied to God, *we know who we are* and that fact, grounded in goodness, worthiness, and hope, fuels movement forward and embraces the joyful possibilities of what "can be." Perhaps this is why Jesus says, "If you remain in my word, you will truly be my disciples, and you will know the truth, and the truth will set you free" (John 8:31-32). The human/divine context sets us free to be who we really are.

On my own journey, I felt that freedom. These are some journal entries while sitting with God in one of my favorite places, the chapel at our church:

> * *I love it here. It is God and I. No worries about whether I am too emotional - or not emotional enough. No worries about the way I act,*

what I say, and how it may impact someone else. I am who I am - no explanation necessary, no apology needed. And who I am is loved. That love gives me strength to be who I am and to do what I am to do. So I am here, God, with you as my rock, to find my grounding in you because only with you can I be truly free.

* *Here in the chapel I am restored. The bells bring calm and hope. The quiet brings rest. And Jesus brings comfort. Life is so overwhelming. I feel like I will collapse from sheer exhaustion. Carry me, Jesus. My heart feels so heavy. Please just give me strength. I know you will. I can rest in here with you. I will find my way. You will guide me.*

* *I breathe you in, God, and I exhale you to the world. Help me to live my life for you. I will focus on your love and pray that your grace will lead me where I need to go. Help me, Jesus, to stay connected to you - your cross, your resurrection, and everything in between.*

* *Once again, I leave the chapel with a "new" attitude that empowers me to tackle the problems at hand and know that with God, all things are possible.*

Freedom in God doesn't mean life is easy. But freedom in God does mean that infinite possibilities exist, and we have the opportunity to participate in God's creative power to transform those possibilities into reality. We are not "things" to be controlled by others or to be haphazardly tossed about by the circumstances of our lives. We are not things who are lifeless, powerless, and robotic. Instead, we know who we are in God, and vitality courses through our veins as we think, feel, imagine, intuit, pray, reflect, contemplate, hope, make choices, take action, and persevere - as we push and pull, demand and yield - as we exercise both freedom and responsibility. Our lives are valuable, meaningful, and significant, simply because God deems them so.

When that fact is not embraced, the consequences are sobering. Viktor Frankl, psychiatrist and Holocaust survivor, states:

> " . . . [T]oday's society is characterized by achievement orientations and consequently it adores people who are successful and happy and, in particular, it adores the young. It virtually ignores the value of all those who are otherwise, and in so doing blurs the decisive difference between being valuable in the sense of dignity and being valuable in the sense of usefulness. If one is not cognizant of this difference and holds that an individual's value stems only from his present usefulness, then, believe me, one owes it only to personal inconsistency not to plead for euthanasia along the lines of Hitler's program, that is to say, 'mercy' killing of all those who have lost their social usefulness, be it because of old age, incurable illness, mental deterioration, or whatever handicap they may suffer."[22]

If the worth of a human being can be bestowed by a human being, then the life of every one of us is bound by the limitations of our humanity and conditioned on the breadth of human vision, the degree of human character, and the capacity for human love. A nihilistic view of humanity that is diminished by confinement, restraint, powerlessness, and meaninglessness is the subject of many artistic and literary works of the 20th century, and Albert Camus' *The Stranger* is one of them. Its central character's aimlessness and unintentionalism leave him disconnected from others and disconnected from his own human power to act:

> * "Maman died today. Or yesterday maybe, I don't know . . . . It occurred to me that anyway one more Sunday was over, that Maman was buried now, that I was going back to work, and that, really, nothing had changed."[23]

---

22 Frankl, V. (1984). *Man's Search for Meaning.* Pocket Books. p. 176.
23 Camus, A. (1988). *The Stranger.* (Ward, M., Trans.). Vintage Books. pp. 3, 24.

* "That evening Marie came by to see me and asked me if I wanted to marry her. I said it didn't make any difference to me and that we could if she wanted to."[24]

* "That's when everything began to reel . . . . My whole being tensed and I squeezed my hand around the revolver. The trigger gave . . . ."[25]

* ". . . [O]f course I had [wished for another life], but it didn't mean any more than wishing to be rich, to be able to swim faster, or to have a more nicely shaped mouth. It was all the same . . . Nothing, nothing mattered."[26]

Camus' character is a powerless object, not much different than a machine. Frankl again:

" . . . I deem it to be a remarkable fact that man, as long as he regarded himself as a creature, interpreted his existence in the image of God, his creator, but as soon as he started considering himself as a creator, began to interpret his existence merely in the image of his own creation, the machine."[27]

If I am a powerless, meaningless, machine-like object, then hope for the future is lost to the emptiness of the present, and suffering and death become vehicles to hopelessness and despair. But hopelessness and despair are not the ends to which we are inherently called. If they were, prisoners would have no need of freedom and the ill would have no need of medical attention. Created in God's image, worthy and good, we are called to life, hope, love, and

---

24 Camus, A. (1988). *The Stranger.* (Ward, M., Trans.). Vintage Books. p. 41.
25 Camus, A. (1988). *The Stranger.* (Ward, M., Trans.). Vintage Books. p. 59.
26 Camus, A. (1988). *The Stranger.* (Ward, M., Trans.). Vintage Books. pp. 119-121.
27 Frankl, V. (1988). *The Will to Meaning.* Penguin Books. p. 16.

goodness, all of which - in pure form - can only be found within the reality of God. There, both life and death take on new meaning and difficulties create life-changing experiences that make us better able to *fully live*. Life becomes the courageous vehicle, not death.

Most certainly I have veered from that path in the many ways I have failed to love. But the hate I have shown and the harm I have caused represent my imperfect humanity, not an imperfect or diminished God. If anything, they indicate just how far I have removed myself from God's goodness and just how intensely I need to seek that goodness once again. If I have the capacity to love and to hate, if I long for the good and suffer from the bad, then humanity alone can never fully satisfy my longings. Only with God will I find the potential for unlimited and joyful possibilities.

CHAPTER FOURTEEN

Love and My Parents

People whose lives reveal unlimited and joyful possibilities move me, inspire me, and change me. My mother and father are two of those people. For the last three years of my mother's life, she was blind and on dialysis. In the last nine months of her life, both legs were amputated, and in the final months of her life, she was losing the use of her hands and fingers because gangrene was beginning to set into those appendages as well.

As she began her journey into the ravages of disease, she - and all of us - had to adjust to the trials of increased limitation. At a wedding dinner, she asked me to tell her where each of the different foods was located on her plate. I recall her trepidation - and the sinking feeling in my stomach, my persistent companion when life's demanding truths challenge me. I remember my mother's grieving process as she relinquished her driver's license. For a woman so active and energetic, this adjustment would certainly require love, patience, and time. But I also remember her earnest expression when our young son climbed onto her lap, book in hand, asking her to read him a story. Although she could do nothing about her limited vision and the necessity of relinquishing a driver's license, she could do something about her grandson's request. She embraced the child who was blind to her blindness and very expressively told him a story from her imagination. Apparently, there is more to our humanity than physical limitation.

* * *

My mother knew how to move past limitation. And she touched people far beyond her family. During one of her hospitalizations, a man came into her room to replace some ceiling tiles. My mother began talking to him as she always talked with those around her. When the hospital personnel took my mother out of the room for a test, the man (whose name my family now knew to be Joe) told my sister that he had to run an errand but would be back. When he returned, he brought with him a thank you card, not a get well card, which read as follows:

> First to tell you thank you
> And then a line to say
> That doing nice things for others
> Just seems to be your way.

He signed the card "Sincerely, Joe" and then wrote this note: "I will say a special prayer for you to God for your speedy recovery to let God know he still has a few angels left on earth to guide us all." That was from someone my mom knew for only fifteen minutes. My mother was a beacon of light during the process of life *and* the process of death. She taught me that the fuel for both journeys is the same: love. Love that strengthens, provides hope, and gathers people in.

* * *

Before my mother's amputations, when my mother was "only" blind and on dialysis, she and my father decided to travel to Las Vegas (a three-hour flight from their home). The fact that my dad hooked my mother up every night to a peritoneal dialysis machine and unhooked her every morning did not seem to faze them; they would just take the machine with them. And the fact that they needed many heavy bags of solution to accomplish this dialysis process was no hindrance either; they would simply have the bags shipped to the hotel.

When they returned home, they never said their trip was difficult. Instead, with much laughter, they told this story: Their hotel room was small and cramped with all the medical equipment, so after breakfast one morning my dad tried to create some space by placing the breakfast tray out in the hall. As he reached out to set the tray down, however, the door closed behind him, and my dad found himself locked out in the hallway - in his underwear. He called to my mom, but being blind and unable to negotiate her wheelchair through the mass of medical equipment, she could be no help. Short of having to go to the front desk scantily clad, but nonetheless with great embarrassment, he did finally find his way back into the room. But remembering the embarrassment, the frustration, and the helplessness only made them laugh more.

I am reminded of two songs from the 1960s. In 1969, Peggy Lee sang "Is That All There Is?" She sang about the fire that consumed her house, the circus she attended, the rejected love of a young man, and she asks if that is all there is to a fire, a circus, and love.[28] While she says that something seems to be missing, she

---

28 Leiber, J., Stoller, M. (1969). Is That All There Is? [Recorded by Peggy Lee.] On *Is That All There Is?* [Record]. Capitol Studios.

seems unable to visualize it, and so she says, "If that's all there is my friends, then let's keep dancing. Let's break out the booze and have a ball if that's all there is."[29]

In contrast, in 1968, in the song "If I Can Dream," Elvis Presley sang that something *must* exist beyond the never-ending difficulties of life: "There must be lights burning brighter somewhere. Got to be birds flying higher in a sky more blue . . . . There must be peace and understanding sometime. Strong winds of promise that will blow away all the doubt and fear."[30] He didn't say we should break out the booze and have a ball; rather, he said, "But as long as a man has the strength to dream he can redeem his soul and fly."[31] Within a larger transcendent reality, although we endure the hardship, we can also dream - and within that intangible vision of something better, humans have the potential to fly.

My mom and dad could have been home, attached and attending to a machine, asking, "Is this all there is?" They could have been immersed in a spiral whose only direction was down. They could have focused on the terrible condition of my mother's body, but chose instead to focus on the excellent condition of her soul. They showed me those intangible qualities that cannot be seen or touched but which are waiting to be unleashed in every human being. They showed me faith, trust, confidence and determination. And in doing so, they soared, taking me and many others with them. No doubt the difficulty was there, but they mastered it and brought Elvis' words to life - because when "[we're] lost in a cloud with too

29 Leiber, J., Stoller, M. (1969). Is That All There Is? [Recorded by Peggy Lee.] On *Is That All There Is?* [Record]. Capitol Studios.
30 Brown, W.E. (1968). If I Can Dream [Recorded by Elvis Presley]. On *If I Can Dream* [Record]. Gladys Music, Inc.
31 Brown, W.E. (1968). If I Can Dream [Recorded by Elvis Presley]. On *If I Can Dream* [Record]. Gladys Music, Inc.

much rain . . . trapped in a world that's troubled with pain . . . as long as a man has the strength to dream he can redeem his soul and fly."[32]

Later, when my mother's legs were amputated and she was getting closer to her death, my father, who had closed the bakery a couple of years before so that he could take care of her, continued to do just that. He fed her, clothed her, got her in and out of her wheelchair, and was her biggest fan. He would hold her hand, look at her, and say, "I don't care what condition you are in. I am happy as long as you are by my side and we are together." He didn't complain that his life had taken a very unexpected path. He didn't give in to limitation and say, "I don't know anything about medicine." Instead, he embraced the possibility of something more, jumped in with both feet, and learned a whole lot about medicine. If anything, he had a renewed vigor, a bigger smile, and a tireless dedication to my mom's well-being. A goodness, a freedom, a love all soaring past human limitation.

And my mother, who certainly had her share of physical problems on which to concentrate, was no less dedicated to my dad's well-being. Recognizing that my dad was only in his mid-sixties, she looked beyond her own suffering and told him that he had a lot of life ahead of him and that she wanted him to remarry after she died.

During the years of my mother's illness, my mother and father both screamed "NO!" to the question "Is that all there is?" They showed me in vivid colors a world I could only know with my heart: a world of selflessness, hope, daring, and courage. A world of *love*, where loving one another consists of self-sacrifice, where others are valued, dignified, and respected for who they are, *as* they are.

---

32 Brown, W.E. (1968). If I Can Dream [Recorded by Elvis Presley]. On *If I Can Dream* [Record]. Gladys Music, Inc.

* * *

In the last months before her death, my mother was totally dependent on those around her; she could not move her body even one inch by herself. Six weeks before her death, we gave her a surprise fifty-seventh birthday party. My blind, kidney-forsaken, and double amputee mother sat next to my dad in a wheelchair with a blanket on her lap. My godmother played the accordion, and we were singing and laughing when someone said, "Speech!" My mother, who never wanted to speak before a group, looked calm and thoughtful. The room became quiet. She began: "You'll pardon me if I don't stand . . . ." There were muted chuckles in the audience, and I remember a feeling of awe that she still had her sense of humor. She then went on to say, "I've been blessed." And she spent five minutes telling us how she had been blessed with wonderful family and friends. I knew that day that if my mother could say she had been blessed, I could get through anything life brought my way. I could get *through*.

* * *

My parents' faithful love could not be undone by suffering. In fact, suffering deepened the roots of that love so that those roots reached to the very depths of their beings. Each of them poured out everything for the other. Two people. One suffering. Together. Transformative love. A powerful hope. All in what lies *beyond*. All in what lies within Jesus' commandments to love God and love neighbor as self.

My parents lived in that beautiful space of love between self and other, between the ravages of a very limited presence and the joyful possibilities of an infinite transcendence. Selflessness drove their actions and love fostered their strength. They had faith in what Jesus promises - that suffering is a conduit for *more*, much more, than the physical reality of bodily limitation. And that "more," that which is clearly and powerfully invisible, fueled the human spirit, transformed limitation into freedom, and greatly expanded reality for all of us. My mother was so much more than a physical body that was decaying and dying in front of us. My father was so much more than a rote response to the stimuli around him. And that power of transcendence does not come from the cells, molecules, and DNA of our physical bodies. It comes from a reality greater than life and death, from the God-given spark of life that lies deep within each one of us.

My parents taught me that life can be meaningful, purposeful, and whole, even when the physical body seems useless and fragmented. They taught me that the human spirit has the power to embrace possibility and change fear to hope, stagnation to inspiration. When my mother felt that she could no longer possibly do any good, she nonetheless continued the fight. And because she did, she taught me more in the last three years of *her* life than she had taught me in the first eighteen of mine. The work of her life continued, and more often than not she taught by *being* rather than doing.

We cannot reduce the behavior of my mother and father to logical premises and conclusions. The essence of their behavior lies within the power of becoming, within the seed of potential, within a power waiting to be unleashed and a promise ready to be fulfilled.

In every suffering lies a profound lesson: that no limitation can ever impede the power of a life created in the image of God.

* * *

For the first nine months after my mother died, I was concerned that my dad would die of a broken heart. But he did not. He did get married again - to another wonderful woman who also showed us that love can be beautifully inclusive. For twenty-five years we have enjoyed a caring and loving extended family with whom we continue our life's journey and our memories of my mother. Joyful possibilities becoming reality once again.

CHAPTER FIFTEEN

World War II

The power of love and goodness often shines brightest in times of human suffering, in times of human tragedy. The courageous acts of first responders and the care, concern, and kindnesses of those who supply food, makeshift shelters, and medical equipment are all evidence that life and love are restored through death. Many of the concentration camp stories in Viktor Frankl's book, *Man's Search for Meaning*, inspire me, but one of my favorites is the story of a fellow prisoner who had stolen potatoes from the potato store. The camp authorities threatened the prisoners that all food would be withheld for a day if they were not told the name of the "thief." Frankl writes: "Naturally the 2,500 men preferred to fast."[33] What is remarkable to me is that these men looked at who they were: starving, emaciated prisoners in a concentration camp, but saw, instead, the possibility of who they could become: honorable men who retained the power to act for a greater good. They were not reduced to their material stomachs; they were elevated to their spiritual potential.

And Raoul Wallenberg's World War II efforts to save Hungarian Jews from death is captivating. His powerful human spirit moved and empowered the human spirit of others. He wanted the Jewish people to see beyond their present situation and imagine a different reality. He said, "Only [when you believe that you can survive] can

---

33 Frankl, V. (1984). *Man's Search for Meaning*. Pocket Books. p. 102.

you do the things necessary to save yourselves"[34] and his impact was startling:

"The slumped backs became a little bit straighter. Those who had managed to squirrel away a bit of meat or cheese started now to distribute it, precious slice by precious slice, among their neighbors."[35]

Holocaust survivor Susan Serena Tabor recalls how Wallenberg's love, care, and kindness moved her to action:

" . . . [B]ecause of Raoul Wallenberg's compassion and concern, hope returned to my soul. With hope came courage. I grabbed my mother's hand and pulled her from the stable floor. As those few women with the safe pass walked out with Raoul Wallenberg, we joined them. When they climbed onto the back of the Swede's truck, we ran into the woods and returned to Budapest on foot."[36]

Beyond the degradation, death, and despair, Wallenberg could see life, dignity, and respect. He helped others have that vision too. *And that vision created a tangible new reality*: by the end of the war, " . . . with inspired courage and creativity he [had] saved the lives of tens of thousands of men, women, and children . . . ."[37] *Death does not have the power to eradicate love or goodness because they are generated in the infinite space of God.* How could the human spirit ever exist within the limited and contained reality of humanity alone?

---

34 Steinhouse, C. (2002). *Wallenberg is Here!* Authorhouse. p. 117. See Bibliography for further information.

35 Marton, K. (1982). *Wallenberg.* Random House. p. 6.

36 Wallenberg, R. (1995). *Letters and Dispatches.* (Board, K., Trans.). Arcade Publishing, Inc. p. 283.

37 *US Congressman and Wallenberg Foundation co-founder Tom Lantos at the United Nations.* (2008, Jan 30). The International Raoul Wallenberg Foundation. Retrieved June 2020, from https://www.raoulwallenberg.net/news/us-congressman-wallenberg/

From where would it gain its freedom to transcend limitation and embrace pure good and selfless love? Evidenced in the action of all these courageous people is an embrace of freedom, not limitation.

* * *

But we must also be mindful of the fact that we don't always seek access to that pure, unwavering love and goodness; sometimes we remain chained to our humanity and its limitations - and within those limitations, hate is powerfully destructive. The Nazi project of death is an example of the depths to which our humanity can fall. In his memoirs, Rudolf Höss, commandant at Auschwitz, described his priorities and his buried emotions:

> "I didn't want to admit my sensitivity . . . The black uniform had become too precious to me and I didn't want to take it off in this way. If I admitted that I was too soft for the SS, I would have been expelled, or at least been dismissed without ceremony. I did not have the heart for that . . . I wanted to have the reputation of being hard. I did not want to be thought of as a weak person . . . I didn't want this situation to get the best of me. My ambition would not permit it . . . I had to be like steel - colder, harder, and even more merciless toward the misery of the prisoners. I saw everything clearly, often too clearly, but I could not allow feelings to overcome me . . . Winning the war was the final goal; the rest didn't matter."[38]

He described his thought process and his powerlessness:

> "Of course, this order was something extraordinary, something monstrous. However, the reasoning behind the order of this

---

38 Höss, R. (1996). *Death Dealer: The Memoirs of the SS Kommandant at Auschwitz.* (Pollinger, A., Trans.). Da Capo Press, Inc. pp. 95-96, 122, 153.

mass annihilation seemed correct to me. At the time I wasted no thoughts about it. I had received an order; I had to carry it out. I could not allow myself to form an opinion as to whether this mass extermination of the Jews was necessary or not . . . I had to bury all my human inhibitions as deeply as possible. In fact, I have to confess openly that after such conversations with Eichmann these human emotions seemed almost like treason against the Führer. There was no escaping this conflict as far as I was concerned. I had to continue to carry out the process of destruction. I had to experience the mass murder and to coldly watch it without any regard for the doubts which uprooted my deepest inner feelings."[39]

And about an execution, he said this:

"I stepped back and gave the order to fire. He collapsed, and I gave him the *coup de grace* to the head . . . I had been so busy during the preparations for the execution that it was only afterwards that I fully realized what had taken place."[40]

In Höss, every possibility met with limitation, so all movement toward a greater good was gridlocked. He was an object in the hands of his superior, a man who was his god: "As leader of the SS, Himmler's person was sacred. His fundamental orders in the name of the Führer were holy."[41] When a human is made into a god, the linear world of human limitation is made dangerously real. When dignity and worth are conditional and no longer inherent to life, our humanity is no longer humane.

---

39 Höss,R. (1996). *Death Dealer: The Memoirs of the SS Kommandant at Auschwitz.* (Pollinger, A., Trans.). Da Capo Press, Inc. pp. 153, 163.
40 Höss, R. (1996). *Death Dealer: The Memoirs of the SS Kommandant at Auschwitz.* (Pollinger, A., Trans.). Da Capo Press, Inc. p. 99.
41 Höss, R. (1996). *Death Dealer: The Memoirs of the SS Kommandant at Auschwitz.* (Pollinger, A., Trans.). Da Capo Press, Inc. p. 153.

Certainly, none of us knows what we would do if we found ourselves in a similar situation. This is the domain of martyrs and saints. But if, as Aristotle says, the virtues are found in between the extremes and require that we behave virtuously in order to become virtuous,[42] then, at a minimum, we must attempt to live our lives in ways that provide practice in walking through the contrasts to that very difficult "in between," all with the confidence that we will become strong enough to transcend self and embrace a greater good when called to do so.

'

---

42 Aristotle. (2004). *The Nicomachean Ethics*. (Thomson, J.A.K., Trans.). Penguin Books.

CHAPTER SIXTEEN

Transcendence

Transcendence, a "moving beyond," is a beautiful experience of human life which connects us to a space beyond our materiality. Art forms such as painting, sculpture, dance, music, theatre, and cinema are some of the many ways that human beings tap into a creative power that expands horizons beyond self and time. It is here that humans often experience "beauty."

Many years ago when I traveled to Rome to pray in the churches, I felt the beauty around me. In St. Peter's Basilica my eyes immediately went up. The ceilings were so high and there was so much beauty to look at on the walls. I was surrounded by altars, tabernacles, chapels; everywhere, I saw biblical characters and artistic renditions of biblical events. Everywhere I saw God, and everywhere I felt a unity with Christians who, through the centuries, also saw God in their midst. I felt a unity with all the saints depicted around me and with all those incredible artists who devoted their lives to creating art that would testify for centuries to the glory of God.

I felt God's power. I didn't want to speak; I couldn't speak. What could I possibly say that would be reverent enough for the glorious God whose presence surrounded me? I felt small. Not inadequate. Not lonely. Just small. I felt loved; I felt at home; I felt strengthened. I saw the sadness of the Virgin Mary's face in Michelangelo's Pietá, but I felt the resurrection of Christ in every miraculous tabernacle. I noticed that the church visitors were quiet, reverent, inquisitive.

Some asked others for help in understanding what they were viewing. Some went off to a side chapel to pray. In this sacred space I knew I was important, not because of accomplishments or possessions, but because I am God's creation. And I felt his presence everywhere.

* * *

But sometimes I have a very difficult time releasing myself to art's power of transcendence. I tend to stay within the confines of analysis and logic - so I stand before a painting and analyze the artist's technique, or I listen to classical music and analyze the instrumentation. I allow myself to think but not feel.

Before I left on the trip to Italy, my spiritual advisor tried very hard to teach me how to let the art of Rome touch a place much deeper in my soul. He asked me if I ever wrote or read poetry. My answers were "no" and "not very often." This is how he guided me: He said that God is speaking to my soul *to act.* I must see God *within me* - not in front of me - and I must enter the world of mystery. In this world, logic is not helpful. I must release myself of words and all prior images and allow the artwork, the mystery, to speak to me and saturate me. Then and only then was I to pick up paper and pen to write. I said I would think about it; he said he figured as much.

I had a difficult time doing as suggested. I wrote that I was having trouble with mystery, that mystery "is more meaningful when we engage the intellect and try to understand." (Obviously I was in the very early stages of appreciating human connection to art.) But on a couple of occasions, I was able to let go of my need for control, let go of my desire for analysis, and embrace the possibility that my soul could be directly touched by the experience. Overwhelmed, sitting in front of Jesus' crib at Santa Maria Maggiore, I wrote:

Your crib, my cries
Poor wood, gilded gold
Your humanity, your divinity
My need, my heart
My ache, my longing
Your forgiving, my taking.

Blood in birth, blood in death
Reign in heaven
Water down to earth.

Teary, reverent, speechless, longing
Humble wood encased in gold
Unpolished wood - like a deck in need of painting
Made perfectly worthy by your touch.
Your gift.
Gold. Red. Blood. Heart. Intelligence.
Your unified path that connects all.

And sitting before the chains that held Peter at San Pietro in Vincoli, I wrote:

Peter's endurance
Peter's humanity
Peter's denial of Christ.
Christ names Peter the rock, the foundation, of his Church.
Christ's mercy
Peter's heart
My hope.

My spiritual advisor helped me experience art in a way I had never before experienced it. On the plane ride home, remembering the process of letting the words flow directly from my heart through my pen without the filter of my thoughts, I remembered the act of writing but had no recollection of the writing's content. With anticipation, I opened my journal - only to discover that all the words were written in English, except one that was written in Italian. That word was *insieme*, the Italian word for "together." In fact, "together" would define the work that lay ahead of me. I would learn to connect my head together with my heart. I would learn to find an "in between" place where I would bring the contrasts together. I would learn that we connect with each other best when we build each other up and travel our journeys of life together.

* * *

Music's transcendent power can also move me deeply, and Ennio Morricone's "Gabriel's Oboe" (as performed by Henrik Chaim Goldschmidt and the Faroe Islands Philharmonic Orchestra) is one example.[43] After listening to it, I wrote:

"I was wrapped in the embrace of this beautiful oboe that richly and resonantly told the story of life: the ordinary, the resigned, the passionate, and most of all, the longing for something more. The music had nothing to do with my conscious thought or my everyday movements, yet it was not an escape or a daydream or imagination. I can neither explain its power nor predict its occurrence, but I always want more of it. It connects to that place within me that is most personal and most hidden, to that place of being, to that place which offers me some pure truth."

---

43 Morricone, E. (1986). Gabriel's Oboe [Performed by Henrik Chaim Goldschmidt and the Faroe Islands Philharmonic Orchestra]. On *The Mission* [Film]. Virgin Records.

Several months later, I decided to listen to this music again, but this time I would do as I had been directed to do in Rome many years before. I would let the music move me and then write only from my heart:

> *Direct arrow oboe*
> *Piercing my heart with its sound.*
> *Heart opened and bleeding*
> *Longing to connect*
> *To a source with only the essentials,*
> *To a oneness that envelops me, embraces me, protects me.*
> *A longing to breathe in this air of life and never let it go.*
> *Not an end to be named, only an end to be felt.*
> *Not an unattended journey but a journey home.*
> *Like a magnet pulled to the iron*
> *Like a butterfly emerging from its chrysalis*
> *This is my purpose.*

The words do not have to constitute good poetry to illustrate the difference between listening intently with my brain and feeling intensely with my heart. The language of the two is different: One is objective observation and the other subjective participation; one is intelligible and the other perceivable; one is accomplished even in detachment and the other only with engagement and closeness.

* * *

Presence and transcendence constitute yet another beautiful juxtaposition in our humanity, and in a journey of faith, that juxtaposition is crucial. If we know the "image of God" through intellect alone, we will be content with an image that is separate and detached. But if we know the "image of God" through the heart's ability to feel, then the "image of God" will mean a gathering-in, a closeness, and a unity - and it will require much more of us.

If God is to return to a meaningful place in our lives, he will not return via cold, impersonal precepts and principles that limit his meaning to rules of logic. Rather, he will return via his mysterious, yet very real, love, mercy, forgiveness, fidelity, and strength. He will return when his mystery is perceived and received. Perhaps this is the reason priest and theologian Karl Rahner said, "The Christian of the future will be a mystic or will not exist at all."[44] Being a mystic does not mean we abandon our rational skills. It means we acknowledge and appreciate that at some point in a conversation about God, the rational must be left behind in order to fully embrace the mysterious. Religious historian Karen Armstrong notes:

"Socrates, Plato, and Aristotle, the founders of Western rationalism, saw no opposition between reason and the transcendent. They understood that we feel an imperative need to drive our reasoning powers to the point where they can go no further and segue into a state of unknowing that is not frustrating but a source of astonishment, awe, and contentment."[45]

44 O'Hearn, B. (2015, June 8). *Karl Rahner.* Western Mystics. https://westernmystics.wordpress.com/2015/06/08/karl-rahner/
45 Armstrong, K. (2010). *The Case for God.* Anchor Books. p. 319.

CHAPTER SEVENTEEN

Our Resistance

Yet rather than embrace a state of unknowing with astonishment, awe, and contentment, I often respond to it with fear. I don't like mystery's requirement that I "let go," so I revert to my controlling tendencies and try to solve an infinite number of "what if" questions. Rather than allow myself to be enveloped in wonder, I hold firm to what I know and can control.

The story of Peter wanting to walk on water is a good example of turning away from wonder:

" . . . [Jesus] came toward them, walking on the sea. When the disciples saw him walking on the sea they were terrified. 'It is a ghost,' they said, and they cried out in fear. At once [Jesus] spoke to them, 'Take courage, it is I; do not be afraid.' Peter said to him in reply, 'Lord, if it is you, command me to come to you on the water.' He said, 'Come.' Peter got out of the boat and began to walk on the water toward Jesus. But when he saw how [strong] the wind was he became frightened; and, beginning to sink, he cried out, 'Lord, save me!' Immediately Jesus stretched out his hand and caught him, and said to him, 'O you of little faith, why did you doubt?'" (Matt 14:25-31).

Worthy of note is the fact that Peter, enveloped in Jesus' protective words to not be afraid, was *not* afraid, asked to walk on water, and *did* walk on water. He grasped the miraculous powers of the Divine. But how quickly he was thrown off course by the strong winds that frightened him and brought him back to the laws of gravity that govern this material world. I have to ask myself: How many times on my journey has God called me to something more - and how many of those times have life's trials, my fear, or my doubt caused me to sink?

One of my favorite stories from Scripture comes from the Second Book of Kings. It is a story about Naaman, a highly esteemed army commander, who is also a leper. Looking for a cure, he finds his way to the prophet Elisha who sends Naaman this message: "Go and wash seven times in the Jordan, and your flesh will heal, and you will be clean" (2Kgs 5:10). Naaman becomes angry at the prophet's direction, saying:

> "I thought that he would surely come out and stand there to invoke the Lord his God, and would move his hand over the spot, and thus cure the leprosy. Are not the rivers of Damascus . . . better than all the waters of Israel? Could I not wash in them and be cleansed?" (2Kgs 5:11-12).

Upset that the prophet did not act as he had expected, sure that he could do anything in the rivers of his homeland that he could do in the river Jordan, sure that he knew what a real prophet would do - even though he was not a prophet himself - Naaman walks away, rejecting the prophet's directive. Naaman *thinks he knows*, but he doesn't, and his limited knowledge prevents him from experiencing the wonder and possibility of the prophet's cure. In another irony, it is Naaman's servants who eventually convince him to do as the prophet directed. He does - and is made clean (2Kgs 5:14).

Whenever I read this passage, I try to reflect on the times I have been a complete know-it-all, the times when the direction I receive from others is so ridiculous in my mind that I pay no attention to it. Are my expectations really so dominant that there is never room for the element of surprise? Do I really think I have that much control and power? I have discovered that when I think I am the only one with vision, it is usually then that my vision is most impaired.

Who am I as a human being? I am a stubborn adherent to what I think I know, a stubborn adherent to a closed and limited reality, and a stubborn rejector of the astonishment, awe, and contentment that is joyfully possible in God.

CHAPTER EIGHTEEN

The Power of Jesus' Life

But Jesus' life, death, and resurrection turn everything into a joyful possibility. He showed us how to live and die as a human. Perhaps that would have been enough to give us strength to persevere - but God nonetheless gave us more. Jesus not only died; he rose after three days. Not only did he endure death, he conquered it, and death no longer has a gripping vise; rather, it has become a mere passageway to something more, something greater, something preeminent. What more could we possibly want?

Jesus' life, death, and resurrection, *if we really believe them*, should change our entire lives into lives of hope and joyful expectation. Jesus' life provides for us the joyful possibility that in spite of our pride, anger, jealousy, and desire for power, we can begin to live our lives differently and realize all that Jesus' death and resurrection promise. Jesus embraces the whole of our existence. He is the infinite God and the finite man. He is the present: life on earth with its joys and sorrows. He is the future: life reunited with the "Absolute Ultimate."[46] Because of his total embrace, we can live within the confines of the finite and also grasp the possibilities of infinity.

---

46 This term was used by Father Alfred Delp in an Advent homily preached in Munich in 1941. Delp, A. (2006). *Advent of the Heart*. (Walburg, A., Trans.). Ignatius Press. p. 39.

Cancer-suffering Christian Wiman beautifully describes being the recipient of an empathic kindness that embraces such a God-like possibility:

> "And I remember when we parted [Wiman and the preacher from a nearby church] there was an awkward moment when the severity of my situation and our unfamiliarity with each other left us with no words, and in a gesture that I'm sure was completely unconscious, he placed his hand over his heart for just a second as a flicker of empathic anguish crossed his face. It sliced right through me. It cut through the cloud I was living in and let the plain day pour its balm upon me. It was, I am sure, one of those moments when we enact and reflect a mercy and mystery that are greater than we are, when the void of God and the love of God, incomprehensible pain and the peace that passeth understanding, come together in a simple human act."[47]

As human beings, each one of us has the power to grasp God's love and reflect a mercy and mystery greater than our humanity. That is the capacity of a human being created in the image of God.

---

47 Wiman, C. (2013). *My Bright Abyss.* Farrar, Straus and Giroux. p. 69.

CHAPTER NINETEEN

The Necessity of Challenging Our Vision

But challenging our vision is absolutely necessary. That is why I love two books written by Father Greg Boyle about his work with gangs over three decades. *Tattoos on the Heart* and *Barking to the Choir* have challenged my perception of gang members and have expanded the breadth of my vision. That doesn't mean that I condone gang violence or gang behavior; it only means I can now better appreciate the reasons gang members find their way to that life. It doesn't mean that I have compromised my principles; it means that my views have been expanded, my understanding has been amplified, and the increased breadth has changed me. Father Boyle talks about what love can do to restore authenticity:

> "At Homeboy Industries, we seek to tell each person this truth: they are exactly what God had in mind when God made them and then we watch, from this privileged place, as people inhabit this truth. Nothing is the same again. No bullet can pierce this, no prison walls can keep this out. And death can't touch it - it is just that huge."[48]

Father Boyle and three of the gang members were invited to the White House by First Lady Laura Bush for a conference and dinner. On the plane ride home, a flight attendant asked one of

---

48 Boyle, G. (2010). *Tattoos on the Heart.* Free Press. pp. 192-193.

the young men about his Homeboy Industries shirt and his tattoos, so the young man began telling her about the work that they do at Homeboy Industries and how they had made history the night before by being the first gang members to walk into the White House. When the young man got back to his seat, he told Father Boyle about his conversation and said the flight attendant had cried. Father Boyle responded:

> "Well, *mojo*, whaddya 'spect? She just caught a glimpse of ya. She saw that you are somebody. She recognized you . . . as the shape of God's heart. Sometimes people cry when they see that."[49]

"She recognized you as the shape of God's heart." What a beautiful sentence. How does that happen? I would say it happens when there is authenticity, the true and complete picture of a human being made in the image of God. The human - as is. No hiding, no speculation, no presumption, no conjecture, just raw authenticity in a place where there is no materiality, no worldly, only the pure essence of our humanity. It is the place where souls reflect God's love and God's goodness. The unknown author of *The Cloud of Unknowing* states: "Every rational creature has both the power of knowing and the power of loving. Our Creator endows us with both, but God will forever remain incomprehensible to the knowing power. Through loving power, however, each of us may know God. Love is everlastingly miraculous."[50]

The task for me on this journey of faith has been to let the seed of God within me grow into a living God who accompanies me through life. Instead of trying to be like someone else, instead of

49 Boyle, G. (2010). *Tattoos on the Heart.* Free Press, p. 205.
50 Bangley, B. (Ed.). (2006). *The Cloud of Unknowing.* Paraclete Press. p. 9.

trying to make other people like me, I have had to learn to allow God to make all of us more *like him.* And God's grace has enabled it to be so: "We arrive by grace where we cannot go by nature."[51] Through God's grace, my vision has been expanded to see beyond myself to the light that shines on all, and that movement has lengthened and broadened my embrace. How it happens is a mystery; *that it happens* is my testimony.

---

51 Bangley, B. (Ed.). (2006). *The Cloud of Unknowing.* Paraclete Press. p. 19.

CHAPTER TWENTY

What Message of Jesus Do I Speak with My Life?

In Pope Francis' Apostolic Exhortation on the Call to Holiness in Today's World, he wrote:

> "May you come to realize . . . the message of Jesus that God wants to speak to the world by your life. Let yourself be transformed. Let yourself be renewed by the Spirit, so that this can happen, lest you fail in your precious mission. The Lord will bring it to fulfillment despite your mistakes and missteps, provided that you do not abandon the path of love but remain ever open to his supernatural grace, which purifies and enlightens."[52]

My life is supposed to speak a message of Jesus to the world. I am called to the authenticity required to fulfill my mission on earth. So what message of Jesus *do* I speak to the world with my life? If I profess faith in Jesus, then what I think, what I say, what I do, all reflect who Jesus is. This is no different, really, than when I remind my children that their actions reflect on their family. So I have to ask myself: What message do I speak with my life?

* When I profess my allegiance to Jesus but make assumptions, make judgments, and exclude my neighbor, do I reflect a Jesus who excludes and turns his back?

---

52 Francis. (2018). *Gaudete Et Exsultate.* Our Sunday Visitor, Inc. p. 18.

* With every angry outburst, every unkind word, every sigh of impatience, have I hidden the luminous God that I am called to reveal?
* Through my inauthenticity, have I inhibited Jesus' love and compassionate presence in the world?
* If faith is anywhere on shaky ground, have my messages of a loveless and intolerant Jesus contributed to its unsteadiness?
* With every hypocritical act, do I hide God's revelatory truth?

I hope that we will consider the message of Jesus that we speak with our lives. I hope that we will face that which is difficult to face and consider how our ability to love is hindered. If we do, I am confident that we will more easily embrace our materiality *and* our spirituality, see ourselves once again in the image of the divine, and see our neighbors in ways we could never before have imagined. But it will require that we relinquish control and rely, instead, on God. C.S. Lewis again:

> "They wanted, as we say, to 'call their souls their own.' But that means to live a lie, for our souls are not, in fact, our own. They wanted some corner in the universe of which they could say to God, 'This is our business, not yours.' But there is no such corner. They wanted to be nouns, but they were, and eternally must be, mere adjectives."[53]

---

53 Lewis, C. S. (1940). *The Problem of Pain.* HarperCollins. p. 75.

Human beings are made in the image of God. Every human limitation has the power to reveal a joyful, divine possibility. Every darkness can be overcome with light. Every bad can be overcome with good. Death is no longer the end but rather a passageway to a new beginning. Slowly but surely, each of us can more fully move toward life, love, light, goodness, and peace. We are all contributing authors to the story of our time. May we each assume our responsibilities and make contributions that amplify God's love and goodness in the world. May we each rediscover and recapture our humanity.

Part IV: My God

My God,
In mystery, you render me helplessly silent.
In love, you render me undeservingly worthy.
You are the gift I receive in gratitude.
You are the gift I desire to share in love.

CHAPTER TWENTY-ONE

Feeling God's Presence

Father Greg Boyle writes: "Not much in my life makes any sense outside of God."[54] The same is true for me. I recently discovered that my journals read like love letters to God. God is no longer "an existence out there." Rather, God is within me, everywhere outside of me, and my connection to everything in existence.

The surprise birthday party that I described in Part I of this book was an example of how experiences of God sometimes come through remarkable personal and meaningful connections.[55] But the first time I had such an experience, in a way that stopped me in my tracks, had to do with my mother. As the travails of her illness were becoming a reality, in the hospital one night she was solemn and silent, not at all herself. The nurse's aide in her room reminded my mother of her own encouraging words to the aide many years before, but the aide's words did not provide impact. Although I vehemently tried, there was nothing I could say or do to lift my mother's spirit. I left that night with a very heavy heart

When I got home, I knelt by the side of my bed and sobbed. I prayed to God with every ounce of my being that he would take my mother's illness away from her and make her well again. I prayed that if curing my mother was not his will, that he would at least send his Holy Spirit to her and give her the strength she needed to endure what she had to endure.

---

54 Boyle, G. (2010). *Tattoos on the Heart*. Free Press. p. 21.
55 See Jung, C.G. (2011). *Synchronicity.* (Hull, R.F.C., Trans.). Princeton University Press.

The next morning, when I walked cautiously into my mother's hospital room, she was sitting up and smiling. I said, "Mom, how are you doing this morning?" and she replied, "Susan, I feel like I have a new spirit about me!" I knew at that moment that God's Holy Spirit was lifting my mother in ways that the aide and I could not do the night before. While my mother's journey ahead was very difficult, she never again lost the strength to endure, and she resumed being the person she had always been: positive, loving, grateful, and concerned about the well-being of others. I used to gasp incredulously at these experiences. Now, I simply smile, acknowledge God's presence, and find a way to express my gratitude.

Similarly, one day when I was trying to work my way through worry and distress, in my mind's eye I suddenly saw letters flowing up into the air. They didn't form words, but simultaneously in my heart I felt and heard what I remembered to be words of a song that we sing at church: "guiding, shielding, sheltering." I repeated those words for about 20 minutes and felt comfort that God was guiding, shielding, and sheltering me.

The next day I was at church for a funeral service and the musicians played the song I had thought about the day before. But the song's refrain was: "God is ever wakeful and always near, watching, shielding, sheltering." Although my memory had not been exact, the words were similar enough to affirm that God was indeed watching, guiding, shielding, and sheltering me. And then our priest's remarks during the service were all about "letting go." I knew that I had to stop relying so much on myself, let go of the worry, and open myself to God's loving embrace.

Early in my spiritual journey, I tried too hard to experience God and only ended up with my own strained and "off the wall" thoughts. It didn't feel right because everything felt contrived. But through the years, as I have felt God's presence more regularly and more profoundly, I have learned that straining to hear God's message or to feel God's presence is not necessary. Actually, the opposite is true: when I feel God's presence, it is often a very easy, soft, and gentle presence that just "comes upon me." It doesn't happen when I am straining to *know;* most often, it happens when I am in fervent prayer - or it happens "out of the blue" as a complete surprise. It happens in quiet humility when I place my humanity within the context of God's divinity. Having felt God's presence so many times is the grounding for my conviction that God is always near.

CHAPTER TWENTY-TWO

Prayer

Prayer is one of those very mystical interactions between God and human beings. Often, I begin praying for something I want God to change, or cure, or "fix" in some way, but the change that results is change within me. Notwithstanding my desire for others to be changed, *prayer changes me.* More journal entries:

* *It was when I cried most and prayed for help that I began to change my thoughts. These changes do not come from my rational mind. In fact, my rational mind was telling me that I could not/should not continue on this path . . . .*

* *Prayer taps into that lifeline of God and creates in me the energy and the courage that I need to deal with the issues that weigh me down. Prayer enables me to better see God in others.*

* *In these trials, I automatically revert to prayer. My soul rises above the hurt as my tears flow. Tears, water from a contained body, pouring and stretching out to the living waters of God. I know my Lord is listening and I am home.*

* *I have known along the way that God has answered my prayer. Until this week, though, I did not realize how profoundly he was answering that prayer. I saw one small part; now I see a bigger picture. Suddenly, my perspective is different - and I am different. These glimpses of*

God's presence help me to see my life in a different context. They help me to realize that much of the curtain still remains closed. Who-what-where-why may all be answered differently when it is opened.

* *Reaching out to God helps to move me past my natural tendencies toward "me, myself, and I." Love is transformative - for the lover and the beloved; it is a beautiful example of God's creative power working in and through us. Because I have been transformed by God's love, I know that we have the power to transform each other with our love.*

* *I am in the chapel. My heart is opened to you, God. Please speak to it:*

There is rhythm in hearing others quietly recite prayer.
Rhythm to my breathing.
Rhythm of my heartbeat.
Someone just walked in and the rhythm is broken.
I was feeling calm but now feel some agitation.
Go back to the rhythm . . . .
Recited prayer ended.
There is noise.
I just received a text.
But now - quiet here again.
A new rhythm is taking shape.
Conversation in church - cleaning/setting up. Work being done.
Spiritual direction in the adjacent room. Work being done.
Quiet in the chapel. Another is reading; I am writing. Work being done.
There is rhythm of work being done.
It is noisier than I like.
The steady rhythm of prayer, heartbeat, no longer heard.
But there is a new rhythm.
This new rhythm of "listen and love" is not the one I would have chosen . . .
But it is the one to which I am led.
It is not what I expected - but it is the reality.
My strong "can do" attitude is learning a softer side.

I am bridging the polarities and it is not easy.
I like it so much better when I am at my strong, "I'll fix it" end.
Perhaps my preconceptions of "strong" must fall too.
It takes more strength for me to be silent than it does for me to fix.
The counter-acting force is hitting me hard.
But it's moving me toward the middle.
If listening and loving are what I now <u>can</u> do,
Even though they feel significantly less than what I <u>want</u> to do -
Then they are what I <u>will</u> do.
I will listen and love. I will listen and love. I will listen and love.
The rhythm of work changes.
I am back to quiet.
Hearing the rhythm of my heartbeat and my breathing once again.
But I am <u>changed</u>.

Prayer also invokes strong connection. More journal entries:

* *I must stay close to the stories. I need to know how to best imitate
Jesus. And I need the strength to hold fast to the hope and promise that
the stories profess.*

* *I stand before your light, bow to you, love you. You calm me. I am
safe - we are all safe - within your love. Help us all to stay connected
to you. You are our answer and our hope.*

* *With you, there is no negativity. There is desire to become better - but
no negativity. Spirit is not hate and fear. It is not arrogant or self-
centered, though it deeply loves and respects self as a beautiful creation
of God. Spirit envelops all with the energy of love and affirmation.*

And the following entry reflects my desire to hold tight but also
my understanding that I must let go:

raa

* *In my heart I am saying, "Make me your instrument." But I hesitate to say it out loud because to ask to be your instrument may mean that I have to travel a very difficult road. Sometimes I say, "Do with me what you will" - but I am fearful of "what you will." So I have to ask myself: Am I in this - or not? I am. So - make me your instrument. Do with me what you will. Help me to live my life to its fullest - for your glory. Help me to see you in all people, in all situations. Help me to latch onto your love and goodness and never let go. Jesus took onto himself everything wrong, everything bad, everything evil, so nothing can harm me. There is nothing for which I should be afraid.*

CHAPTER TWENTY-THREE

The Practice of Religion

Journaling, storytelling, traditions, and patterns help to create a *practice* of religion, practice of a purposeful way of life. And the practice of religion requires just that: practice. Armstrong again:

> "[Religion's] truth was acquired by practical action. It is no use imagining that you will be able to drive a car if you simply read the manual or study the rules of the road. You cannot learn to dance, paint, or cook by perusing texts or recipes. . . . There are some things that can be learned only by constant, dedicated practice, but if you persevere, you find that you achieve something that seemed initially impossible. . . . Religion is a practical discipline that teaches us to discover new capacities of mind and heart. It is no use magisterially weighing up the teachings of religion to judge their truth or falsehood before embarking on a religious way of life."[56]

For me, time dedicated to daily Mass, daily prayer, daily reflection is that practice of religion. Doing the same thing every day provides a space for renewal and a reference point for my actions throughout the day. The practice of religion no longer consists of "things I must do" but rather "things I want to do," and these things are no longer extrinsic and alien to who I am but rather intrinsic and intimate to who I am. When I do not engage in this practice for some reason, I am not freed of an obligation; I am deprived of a

---

56 Armstrong, K. (2010). *The Case for God.* Anchor Books. pp. xii - xiii.

gift. "Practice of God" opens the floodgates for receiving the graces and mercies of God.

I go to church as often as I can because the Mass moves me deeply. When I recite the Memorial Acclamation, "We proclaim your death, O Lord, and profess your resurrection until you come again," the past, the present, and the future come together in one perfect unity. And I receive the Eucharist in thanksgiving and in hope of what this beautiful Eucharistic Prayer envisions: "By the working of your power it comes about, O Lord, that hatred is overcome by love, revenge gives way to forgiveness, and discord is changed to mutual respect."[57]

But it is not only the liturgy that moves me. The Marian Shrine reminds me that Mary believed God's words, said yes to them, and understands profoundly the suffering of a mother's heart. The bells that chime summon me to God and remind me that time is passing and that work is to be done *now*. And their resonance lingers - just as God's presence lingers in my soul - even when my thoughts, words, and deeds deny him.

Those who sit next to me and all around me inspire me in ways they can never know. The weak and the strong, the healthy and the sick, the young and the old, together, in one place of unity. Parents walking up to communion with their children, modeling what is important in their lives. Pregnant women walking up to receive Jesus for themselves and for their babies. Older children bowing down when receiving communion; very young children reaching out, desiring to receive it too. Men and women helping spouses to walk, leading spouses who cannot lead themselves. Those with walkers

---

57 Aymond, G.M. (2011). *The Roman Missal.* Liturgy Training Publications.

or in wheelchairs, at church in spite of their suffering. Those who have lost loved ones, faithfully honoring God notwithstanding their heartache. In church, God is beautifully communal and personal. I am moved, grateful, inspired, and strengthened. I am changed.

The authentic and inherent zest for life that children express at church is revelatory. One of my favorite memories comes from a time when our daughter was about four years old. She insisted that she have her feet washed at Holy Thursday Mass, the Mass of the Last Supper on Thursday before Easter. Unlike the ceremony today at our church when many children participate, my recollection is that at that time, our daughter was the only child at the altar. I watched her sit in the chair, bare feet swinging and toes pointing, as she waited patiently for her turn.

I have often thought about that night - and what it was that moved many of us to tears as we watched her. Perhaps it was her honest, inherent response to God; perhaps it was her expectant encounter with God; perhaps it was her innocent certainty that she *had* to do this. I only know that all these years later, the beauty of it moves me still because I can see how powerful God within us can be - when we embrace his presence, when his presence hasn't been diminished by our reason, our cynicism, and our life experience. Watching our daughter on that Holy Thursday, I only knew that I very much wanted to recapture that God within me.

My favorite church service of the year is the Holy Thursday Mass because Jesus' humanity seems so real as he prepares to die. After that service, while praying before the Eucharist, I always think about the words we sing: "Stay and keep watch with me; watch and pray." They echo Jesus' words in Matthew 26:38: "My soul is sorrowful even to death. Remain here and keep watch with me."

He was facing his impending death - the most unknown event of our human life - and he wanted to have others with him. He wanted them to stay with him - and watch. Watch because something was going to happen. Watch for it - with him. When we humans face difficulty, it is good to have someone by our side, to be with us, to help us face the task. How human Jesus sounds. On Holy Thursday night, I cannot ask Jesus for anything; I cannot burden him. That night, I only want to help him. I only want to stay and keep watch. With him.

* * *

Some say that religion is merely a straw we grasp to make life easy. Actually, the opposite is true: it is a truth we grasp that makes life authentic, selfless, noble, charitable, and humble, all very difficult ends to achieve. Some say that religion is merely one more method of escaping reality. Actually, religion is immersion *into* reality, embracing what is good, requiring self discipline, demanding change, and meeting life's challenges head on, with hope, determination, and perseverance. Living a life of faith takes strength. It means:

* Being alone even in the midst of crowds;
* Being authentic even when authenticity requires a swim upstream;
* Being patient with those who try our patience;
* Standing up for who we are and affirming self within the context of a greater God, even when the surrounding culture negates life and meaning;
* Acknowledging blessing even in the midst of trials;

* Doing for others with no expectation of return;
* Trusting when we would much rather have certainty and restraining when "anything goes" would be so much easier;
* Speaking out when it would be easier to remain silent, remaining silent when we could say so much, and engaging in self-reflection when we *do* say so much;
* Forgiving when we are hurt;
* Giving up control when we want control the most; and
* Working to determine the truth when it is easier to be immersed in conviction.

But a life of faith *is* possible. We must simply choose to live it. "When one is thirsty one quenches one's thirst by drinking, not by reading books which treat of this condition."[58] We must choose to take the drink from God's life-giving waters.

---

58 De Caussade, J.-P. (2014). *Abandonment to Divine Providence.* Ignatius Press. p. 9. See Bibliography for further information.

CHAPTER TWENTY-FOUR

Life's Difficulties

Faith is the conduit to dynamic sustenance and powerful refreshment, especially in times of difficulty. The following are journal entries from some of my difficult days:

* *My teeth hurt so much from always clenching them. My body seems to be in a state of revolt. I have difficulty smiling or talking. I have difficulty even looking at anyone when I walk. I want to just turn into myself. At least for today, no one can help; if anything, though well meaning, they make it worse. Why does it hurt so much? There seems to be so little that matters other than this hurt. It is all-consuming - and I need to make much more room for what is positive. I know that. But it seems that there are times that we have to work through the disequilibrium in order to find the equilibrium once again. The snapshot of today, however, is not a snapshot of every day forward. It will get better. Of that, I am certain. I feel alone - but I am also certain that my God is with me. It is God and I. No more, no less. But I do not need more.*

* *I am making so many mistakes. Please let me feel your presence. Help me, please. I know you are there. I know that what feels so overwhelming right now won't always feel so. Please just give me strength to get through.*

* *It's humbling. It's humbling. It's humbling. I am learning a lot about*

letting go. It is one of the most difficult things I have ever had to do. I must acknowledge that I have no power to change the circumstance in which I find myself. Such an acknowledgment emasculates all ego because ego simply cannot exist amid helplessness. My desires, my rights, my knowledge, my self all tumble away as I cry for help.

* *Not knowing what to do - and wondering if what I do do is the right thing - definitely take me off balance. And it feels really bad. It is unsettling. I just may not be everything I thought I was. It takes me to helplessness - and God. I only know that I ache. I feel like my insides are torn out. It is so hard. I don't know what I am supposed to do, but I will have to learn - and do it. That it is difficult is irrelevant.*

* *Help me, God, to have patience. Help me to see what I am not seeing, to hear what I am not hearing, to feel what I am not feeling, to know what I am not knowing. Take evil, please, from my heart and replace it with as much of your love and goodness as a human can possibly hold. Help me to focus on others - not me. Help me to persevere. Help me to feel more centered again.*

* *There is a pain so deep within me that it renders me silent. Even if I try to speak, nothing comes out. The pain makes me angry. I feel like no one can possibly understand. I look at the beautiful sky and although I see it, and can say that it is beautiful, I am numb to it; I am no longer moved by it. The pain is too great; the pain has taken over. Many times I have written about God's nearness and God's presence. Tonight I write of his intangibility. Many times I have written about God's messages to me. Tonight I write about his silence. Many times I have written about the transformative and healing power of our love for one another. Tonight, I write that only God has the power to heal. I don't know how to pray right now. I just give it all up to God.*

CHAPTER TWENTY-FIVE

Messages of Hope and Possibility

But during my darkest days, I received five spiritual messages of hope and possibility. I wrote them. I read them. I recalled them often. They gave me the strength to endure because they housed five possibilities to which I learned to cling.

Joy

The message of joy came in an unusual manner, and it came at a church in Detroit during the closing Mass of a National Christ Child Society convention. Before Mass began, I had been earnestly praying, most especially for my children, and had been reflecting on the mural of Jesus the Good Shepherd that was on the wall behind the altar. The music began, the priests processed to the front of the church, and then four things happened to me simultaneously:

* All the people around me were suddenly motionless and "frozen" in place;
* A pulsating but stationary white light, repeatedly bursting open like a white starlike firework, appeared at the top left corner of the mural;
* I felt an overwhelming sense of joy, absolutely unlike any feeling I have ever had, with a sense that this kind of joy can only be experienced in the life to come; and

* The words that immediately came to my mind were these: "This is what it is going to feel like when I see my mother again!"

And then it was over. What I had seen and felt disappeared, the priest was talking, and the people around me were once again moving. I had never had an experience like that before, and it moved me to the core. I felt the connections between my mother and me, my children and me, all of us and the Christ Child. I felt a connection between stillness and pulsating light, between this life and the next. And I felt the overwhelming joy that enveloped the entire experience. By the time my mother's favorite song, "Amazing Grace," was sung later in the Mass, I was well aware of God's amazing graces. I knew that God's message of joy housed the possibility that no matter how difficult a situation, there is opportunity for wonder and elation.

Companionship

In the pool at my community's recreation center one morning, praying fervently once again, the scent of roses overtook me. I stopped - and asked the two other women in the pool if they smelled the same thing. They did not. To me, the fragrance was very strong and very beautiful.

Doing research about the scent of roses when I got home, I learned that Padre Pio, the Italian saint who suffered the "stigmata," the marks of Jesus' crucifixion, was one of the saints associated with the scent of roses. The association of roses with Padre Pio was another of those mystical but meaningful connections in my life. Not long before that, I had learned about Padre Pio, but my journey to him had gotten off to a slow start. Years before, a friend had given me a bag of books about him which I returned to her, unread, many months later. I never thought about the saint again until another friend gave me a small Padre Pio keepsake. It seemed that Padre Pio was crossing my path enough to prompt further inquiry, so I bought a book and began to read about his life. I developed great admiration for him, the suffering he endured, and the supernatural gifts with which he was endowed. When I learned after my pool experience that his miracles were associated with the scent of roses, the pieces all fell into place for me - and I sensed that I was receiving another message of possibility: that the saints would always walk with me and that I would find strength through companionship.

Light

I was praying in our home one evening. The three alcoves in the wall behind me were situated next to each other horizontally, and each one was lit. At some point during my prayers, the brightness of the light dimmed, so I turned around to see what had happened. The middle alcove light had gone out but the lights in the two end alcoves remained lit. I could see well enough to continue reading my prayer book (a Padre Pio prayer book), so I did, but about thirty to forty-five seconds later, the middle light came back on and never went out again until we had to change the bulb several months later. I took that as a sign that light always surrounds the darkness and that light will always prevail over the darkness. God's message transmitted the possibilities of illumination, radiance, and broader vision.

Love and Prayer

On a day when I really needed to be lifted up, a stranger (whose name I learned to be Mary) told me that love would make everything fine. Her message was God's gift to me that day. Her message helped me envision the possibility of love's transformational healing. And on another day of great anguish, a priest friend told me to never underestimate the power of prayer and to know that good would come from what I do. His message affirmed that prayer elicits God's graces which create infinite possibilities for goodness.

* * *

God's messages of joy, companionship, light, love, and prayer were all about hope; I held fast to their confident thrust. When the trials of the day weakened my hold, I clutched them and read them over and over and over again. Doing so reduced my angst and shaped my energies into expressions of love, love which turned possibilities into realities. I needed only to trust in God's words: "If you have faith the size of a mustard seed, you will say to this mountain, 'Move from here to there,' and it will move. Nothing will be impossible for you" (Matt 17:20).

My spiritual journey has brought me to a place of peace - not because life is easy or effortless, not because I am never overwhelmed, but because no matter how bad it may seem, the God of joy and love will unfailingly accompany me and illuminate the way to goodness.

CHAPTER TWENTY-SIX

Burning and the Holy Spirit

One day in the chapel of our church, I looked intently at the spire's lit candle. I watched the flickering flame. But hidden from my view was the flame's shadow on the floor. When I noticed it, I saw not only the shadow of the flame but also the shadow of the flame's smoke that was furiously moving up and out, beyond the candle's glass holder. Nowhere to be seen when I looked directly at the candle but everywhere to be seen when I looked at the candle's shadow on the floor, that image of the smoke's movement remains with me as an image of the Holy Spirit, God's continuing presence in our world: invisible, yet moving away from its source into the world to bring God to each and every one of us.

Looking directly at the candle, I saw the back-and-forth movement of the flickering flame, but I could not see the fruit of that flame, the smoke. I am reminded that on my journey, although I always wanted tangible results, I had to learn to trust that God's mysterious works are fruitful, whether or not I can tangibly embrace them. Interesting also is the fact that only in the darkness of the shadow could I see the full *direction* of the movement - not only the "back and forth" of the flame but also the "up and out" of the smoke. Certainly it is true that on my journey, darkness housed many of the lessons that ultimately provided me with direction.

The Holy Spirit has evoked a "burning" within me: a yearning, an unceasing desire for "something more,"and with it has come a burning and painful transformation. Thomas Merton, in the famous last page of his book *The Seven Storey Mountain*, talks about the "burnt men" whose pain and rejection lead them to Christ's "anguish and . . . poverty."[59] Henri J. M. Nouwen, in his book *With Burning Hearts*, talks about the burning hearts of those who traveled with Jesus on the road to Emmaus.[60] And Rumi, the 13th century Sufi mystic and poet, provides perfect imagery for my experience of God's movement within me when he writes of a candle with the words "diminish," "burn," "melt," and "become light and heat."[61] Transformation is not easy, and it is often painful, but the candle's fire is not only witness to the hurt, it is also witness to the change that yields something beautiful and new: heat that warms and light by which we can more lovingly see.

Close to a candle's flame is hot, melted liquid; far from the flame is cold, stagnant solid. If the Spirit is that fire, that flame, I don't want to be the stagnant solid; I want to be in that hot, moving liquid of change. There, like the purification of silver and gold, my impurities can be separated and discarded while my essence is embraced and strengthened. There, like the purification of silver and gold, I can be in the fire without being consumed by the fire. Jesus baptizes "with the holy Spirit and fire" (Matt 3:11) and somehow, through the grace of God, the Spirit's fire has emblazoned my soul with a burning desire for God - and that desire has made the fire bearable.

---

59 Merton, T. (1948). *The Seven Storey Mountain*. Harcourt, Inc. p. 462.
60 See Nouwen, Henri. (1994). *With Burning Hearts*. Orbis Books.
61 Rumi. (2010). *The Big Red Book*. (Barks, C., Trans.). HarperCollins. p. 92.

CHAPTER TWENTY-SEVEN

My God

I find God when I go deep into the most quiet, still parts of my being. There, in the essence of who I am, I find my steadfast core, the eternal fixed presence, the seed, always waiting and expectant. There, in the essence of who I am, I find the presence that beckons me to growth and that, if I allow it, brings new life within me. There, in the essence of who I am, I find the root that requires stillness and the stem that requires a willingness to *become*.

There, in that deepest center of my being, I long for God, and in the quiet longing of my soul, I find God. An invisible reality, a nameless "nudge." A God like nothing I can possibly express, but a God whose transcendent, ineffable reality gives context and meaning to my humanity. A God whose mercy, grace, generosity, and love demand my mercy, grace, generosity, and love. A God who is present at the end of my seeking, loving at the end of my hating, merciful at the end of my straying. A relentless God, "God the Hound,"[62] to be sure. A God whose essence is with me wherever I go, never a hindrance but always the advocate, never a stranger but always the companion. A God who demands advocacy and companionship from me. A God I seek on a walk, driving a car, sitting in front of the Tabernacle in the chapel of my church. A God whose expectations are excruciatingly high. A God whose

---

62 See Thompson, F. (2000). *The Hound of Heaven and other poems.* International Pocket Library.

love is infinitely higher. A God who jostles my mediocrity and commands my excellence. A God whose Spirit embraces me while propelling me to newness and change. A God who turns my despair into strength, who turns my doubt into faith, who provides hope in another tomorrow. The presence I seek in gratitude, the presence I seek in anger, the presence which repeatedly restores my balance and gives me life. My rock. My grounding. My God.

Conclusion

This writing process has provided me with the luxury of looking backward and weaving my experiences into a story about moving forward. I have come to better appreciate the circle of life, the movement from generation to generation, and the passing of time. My father, my stepmother, and the memory of my mother continue to be my anchor. My husband continues to walk next to me in patient love. And our children extend the reach of the past as they move into the future.

Our son is married to the beautiful young woman to whom he became engaged - and she is a pastry chef. Her conversations with my dad renew our bakery memories, unite us in our love of baking, and connect our family's past with our children's future. And interestingly, our son is a university professor who teaches and does research, and our daughter, a teacher by training, works with children. They continue the work of instructing, shaping lives, tackling problems, and broadening understanding. They had early experience in these matters. I know - because I was their first pupil.

This journey toward God has been remarkably challenging and amazingly beautiful. I had much to learn – and still have much to learn; that is simply the journey of life. But what I have learned has brought me to wholeness and to the "in between" space that is large enough for all of us.

I write this book with the hope that by better knowing our humanity within the context of God's divinity, we will find our way to peace with ourselves and to meaningful relationships with each other. I write this book with the hope that we will more successfully walk this journey of life *together.* And I write this book with the hope that we will embrace our inherent goodness, assume our responsibility, and be transformed by the wonder of joyful possibilities.

Bibliography

Aristotle. (2004). *The Nicomachean Ethics.* (Thomson, J.A.K., Trans.). Penguin Books.

Armstrong, K. (2010). *The Case for God.* Anchor Books.

Aymond, G.M. (2011). *The Roman Missal.* Liturgy Training Publications.

Bangley, B. (Ed.). (2006). *The Cloud of Unknowing.* Paraclete Press.

Boyle, G. (2017). *Barking to the Choir.* Simon & Schuster.

Boyle, G. (2010). *Tattoos on the Heart.* Free Press.

Brown, W.E. (1968). If I Can Dream [Recorded by Elvis Presley]. On *If I Can Dream* [Record]. Gladys Music, Inc.

Camus, A. (1988). *The Stranger.* Vintage Books.

Coetzee, J.M. (1982). *Waiting for the Barbarians.* Penguin Books.

De Caussade, J.-P. (2014). *Abandonment to Divine Providence.* Ignatius Press. This book is currently published by Ignatius Press but the author's copy does not include a publisher's name. The quotation on page 129 was found in Book I, Chapter I, Section 4.

Delp, A. (2006). *Advent of the Heart.* Ignatius Press.

Delp, A. (2004). *Prison Writings.* Orbis Books.

Esquith, R. (2003). *There Are No Shortcuts.* Anchor Books.

Francis. (2018). *Gaudete Et Exsultate.* Our Sunday Visitor, Inc.

Frankl, V. (1984). *Man's Search for Meaning.* Pocket Books.

Frankl, V. (1988). *The Will to Meaning.* Penguin Books.

González-Balado, J. L. (1997). *Mother Teresa - Her Life, Her Work, Her Message.* Liguori Publications.

Hartdegen, S. O. J., & Ceroke, P. C. C. O. (1970b). *Saint Joseph Fine Art Edition New American Bible* (First Printing ed.). Catholic Book Publishing Co.

Höss, R. (1996). *Death Dealer: The Memoirs of the SS Kommandant at Auschwitz*. Da Capo Press, Inc.

Jung, C. G. (2011). *Synchronicity*. (Hull, R.F.C., Trans.). Princeton University Press.

Kasper, W. (2011). *Jesus the Christ*. Continuum Books.

Kierkegaard, S. (1971). *Christian Discourses etc.* (Lowrie, W., Trans.). Princeton University Press.

King, M. L. (1988). *The Measure of a Man*. Fortress Press.

Leiber, J., Stoller, M. (1969). Is That All There Is? [Recorded by Peggy Lee]. On *Is That All There Is?* [Record]. Capitol Studios.

Lewis, C. S. (1961). *A Grief Observed*. HarperCollins.

Lewis, C. S. (1940). *The Problem of Pain*. HarperCollins.

Marton, K. (1982). *Wallenberg*. Random House.

Merton, T. (1948). *The Seven Storey Mountain*. Harcourt, Inc.

Morricone, E. (1986). Gabriel's Oboe. [Performed by Henrik Chaim Goldschmidt and the Faroe Islands Philharmonic Orchestra]. On *The Mission* [Film]. Virgin Records.

Nouwen, H. (1994). *With Burning Hearts*. Orbis Books.

O'Hearn, B. (2015, June 8). *Karl Rahner*. Western Mystics. https://westernmystics.wordpress.com/2015/06/08/karl-rahner

Philippe, J. (2020) *About Father Jacques Philippe*. Fr. Jacques Philippe. Retrieved June 2020, from https://www.frjacquesphilippe.com/about

Phillippe, J. (2008). *Called to Life*. Scepter Publishers.

Rosenblatt, N., Horwitz, J. (1995). *Wrestling with Angels*. Delacorte Press.

Rumi. (2010). *The Big Red Book*. (Barks, C. Trans.). HarperCollins.

Steinhouse, C. (2002). *Wallenberg is Here!* Authorhouse. This book is currently published by Authorhouse but the author's copy does not include a publisher's name. The quotation on pages 89-90 was found in Chapter 7 under the subsection "Pest, Offices of the *Judenrat*, a Day Later."

The Empty Chair. (2020). Jaredstory.com. Retrieved June 2020, from http://www.jaredstory.com/empty_chair.html

Thompson, F. (2000). *The Hound of Heaven and other poems.* International Pocket Library.

Tugwell, S. (1980). *The Beatitudes: Soundings in Christian Traditions.* Templegate Publishers.

US Congressman and Wallenberg Foundation co-founder Tom Lantos at the United Nations. (2008, Jan 30). The International Raoul Wallenberg Foundation. Retrieved June 2020, from https://www.raoulwallenberg. net/news/us-congressman-wallenberg/

Wallenberg, R. (1995). *Letters and Dispatches.* (Board, K., Trans.). Arcade Publishing, Inc.

We Heart Mom: Mother's Day Stories from Hallmark Writers. (2015, May 8). ThinkMakeShareBlog. Retrieved June 2020, from https://www. thinkmakeshareblog.com/mothers-day-stories/

Wiman, C. (2013). *My Bright Abyss.* Farrar, Straus and Giroux.